Salvation Is More Complicated Than You Think

A Study On the Teachings of Jesus

Salvation Is More Complicated Than You Think

A Study On the Teachings of Jesus

ALAN P. STANLEY

COLORADO SPRINGS · LONDON · HYDERABAD

Authentic Publishing
We welcome your questions and comments.
USA   1820 Jet Stream Drive, Colorado Springs, CO 80921
      www.authenticbooks.com
UK   9 Holdom Avenue, Bletchley, Milton Keynes, Bucks, MK1 1QR
      www.authenticmedia.co.uk
India Logos Bhavan, Medchal Road, Jeedimetla Village, Secunderabad
      500 055, A.P.

Salvation Is More Complicated Than You Think
ISBN-13: 978–1-934068-02-1
ISBN-10: 1-934068-02-0

Copyright © 2007 by Alan P. Stanley

10 09 08 07 / 6 5 4 3 2 1

Published in 2007 by Authentic
All rights reserved. No part of this book may be reproduced in any form without permission in writing from the publisher, except in the case of brief quotations embodied in critical articles or reviews.

All Scripture quotations, unless otherwise indicated, are taken from the *Holy Bible, New International Version*®. *NIV*®. Copyright © 1973, 1978, 1984 by International Bible Society. Used by permission of Zondervan. All rights reserved. Emphases added are in italics.

Scripture quotations marked ESV are taken from The Holy Bible, English Standard Version, copyright © 2001 by Crossway Bibles, a publishing ministry of Good News Publishers. Used by permission. All rights reserved.

Library of Congress Cataloging-in-Publication Data
Stanley, Alan P.
  Salvation is more complicated than you think : a study on the teachings of Jesus / Alan P. Stanley.
    p. cm.
  ISBN-13: 978-1-934068-02-1
  ISBN-10: 1-934068-02-0
  1. Salvation--Christianity. 2. Jesus Christ--Teachings. I. Title.
  BT751.3.S89 2007
  234--dc22
                    2007041658

Cover and interior design: Luz Design, www.projectluz.com
Editorial team: Mike Morrell, Betsy Weinrich

Printed in the United States of America

To my father-in-law

Who was the first to encourage me to write this book
and has sacrificed much time and money to ensure it got done.

CONTENTS

FOREWORD	ix
PREFACE	xiii
ACKNOWLEDGMENTS	xvii
Chapter One JUST WHO WILL BE SAVED?	1
Chapter Two GRACE AND WORKS: ARE THEY OPPOSED?	21
Chapter Three FAITH AND SALVATION: DO THEY ALWAYS GO TOGETHER?	35
Chapter Four APART FROM ME YOU CAN DO NOTHING	59
Chapter Five I CHOSE YOU TO BEAR FRUIT	87
Chapter Six CAN I BE SAVED AND NOT LOVE OTHERS?	101
Chapter Seven CAN I BE SAVED AND BE WEALTHY?	129
Chapter Eight CAN I BE SAVED AND NOT PERSEVERE?	151
Chapter Nine WILL GOD'S JUDGMENT AFFECT MY SALVATION?	179
Chapter Ten SOME PASTORAL REFLECTIONS	195

FOREWORD

For human beings there is not a more paramount question than what must we do to be saved. This question arises with special urgency in the context of religion, especially within the context of Christianity. If God has called us into existence out of nothing to have fellowship with him as our reason for being then we would do well to find out what he requires of us. Moreover if what is at stake in this present life is whether at its end we shall be granted a permanent, eternal relationship with God, or shall suffer everlasting exclusion from the presence of him who is the sole source of all good, then we would do well to find out what he requires of us.

The Bible lays out a clear answer. But the biblical teaching on salvation is fuller than what is often taught and believed at the popular level in large sectors of the western church.

Ask almost any evangelical what makes them saved, and you will quickly be told Christians are saved by faith, not by works. That is certainly how life in Christ begins. Doesn't John 3:16 say the person who will not perish but have eternal life is the one who "believes" in God's only Son? Doesn't the apostle of Christian liberty say a person is justified "by faith apart from works of law" (Romans 3:28)?

Holding essential salvation to be sealed when people first trust in Jesus, some who are highly motivated go on to pursue "discipleship" for the sake of heavenly rewards. Others, less ambitious, infer that how they live is unimportant and continue to do as they please. "Free from the law, oh, happy condition!" [Now I can sin, and there's no perdition!] (quoted portion from "Once for All" by P. P. Bliss).

Paul, John, and other New Testament authors did not support the interpretation that a godly lifestyle is an optional response to salvation accomplished. Hear them. James: "A person is justified by works and not by faith alone" (James 2:24). Luke: The Gentiles "should repent and turn to God and perform deeds worthy of their repentance" (Acts 26:20). Hebrews: "You need endurance, so that when you have done the will of God, you may receive what was promised" (Hebrews 10:36). Peter: "Make every effort to supplement your faith with virtue . . . for if you do this . . . there will be richly provided for you an entrance into the eternal kingdom of our Lord and Savior Jesus Christ" (2 Peter 1:5, 10, 11).

Paul, for his part, holds that salvation unfolds in stages. We are already in a state of salvation (Ephesians 2:8), but we are also in process of being saved (1 Corinthians 15:2), and we have yet to be saved (Romans 5:9–10). Insofar as final salvation lies before us, we are to work it out with fear and trembling, not in our own strength, but by the grace of God who is at work in us both to will and to do what pleases him (Philippians 2:12–13). What counts toward final justification is faith "working through love" (Galatians 5:6), for "the doers of the law will be justified" (Romans 2:13). "Those who do what is true come to the light, so that it may be clearly seen that their deeds have been done in God" (John 3:21). We will "have boldness on the day of judgment, because as he is, so are we in this world" (1 John 4:17).

The New Testament therefore plainly demands Christian obedience, not mere passivity, in the course of the journey toward salvation. Evidently we need a more biblically nuanced understanding of "works." Not all works are the same; not all are opposed to faith. Some works express and complete faith. Moral efforts of human nature in its sinful state of bondage, apart from God's Spirit (Paul's "works of law") cannot save, because nothing has value that does not flow ultimately from God as its origin. But the fruit of the Spirit is otherwise: "He who sows to the Spirit will from the Spirit reap eternal life" (Galatians 6:8).

Salvation is truly received by faith. But the faith that saves immediately begins through vital union with him to produce such deeds, even if at first it cleaves to the worthiness of the crucified and risen one having no deeds of its own fit for God to accept. Saving faith becomes active as well as receptive; saving righteousness becomes existential as well as imputed. God, at the last judgment, will formally recognize this dynamic energy of the Spirit in believers with a view to welcoming its human agents into the blessings of the age to come. The good news of the gospel is that God takes us as we come and transforms us into what he wants us to be.

So what did Jesus himself, the very fount of Christianity, teach about salvation? Alan Stanley's doctoral thesis at Dallas Theological Seminary (2003) delved into that very question, and concluded on the basis of a wide array of data in the synoptic gospels that works of the latter sort, the practical deeds of righteousness that spring from faith, are of critical importance to anyone who wants to stand justified in the future day of judgment. He revised and published his results in a scholarly monograph, *Did Jesus Teach Salvation by Works? The Role of Works in Salvation in the Synoptic Gospels* (Evangelical Theological Society Monograph Series, 4; Eugene, Oregon: Pickwick, 2006).

Dr. Stanley is not only a well-qualified academic on the faculty of Mueller College of Ministries in Queensland, Australia. He is also an associate pastor and a speaker on the Sunshine Coast, and has a passion to communicate the truth of God's word to our generation. He has taken to the task of revisiting his thoughts to make this key aspect of the gospel as clear as possible for an even wider readership. May I commend to you the present book, *Salvation Is More Complicated Than You Think*. With Dr. Alan Stanley as a reliable guide, I invite you to read, to ponder, to learn, and to respond to our Lord and Savior Jesus Christ in faith and obedience, that you may be saved.

—*Paul A. Rainbow*, D.Phil.,
Professor of New Testament
Sioux Falls Seminary, Sioux Falls, South Dakota

If you want my answer on where I think they will spend eternity I'm not going to give one. I can't—their lives aren't over yet! I include them here because I think they are typical of many people inside and outside of church today.

My guess is that most of us could probably substitute names of people we know for either John, Mary, Bob, or Katie. We may even substitute our own name. We speak of the Bobs and Katies of this world in a number of ways—"they have not gone on for the Lord," "they're not walking with the Lord," "they're out of fellowship," or "they're backslidden." But we would never say that about the John's and Mary's. Why would we? They turn up for church every Sunday and are part of the Christian scene.

But one day it won't matter how we have described people or even ourselves. For we will all stand before God. What will he say to you? Peter tells us to "be all the more eager to make your calling and election *sure*. For if you do these things, you will never fall, and you will receive a rich welcome into the eternal kingdom of our Lord and Savior Jesus Christ" (2 Pet. 1:10–11). Are you making your calling and election sure? John and Mary aren't; Bob and Katie certainly aren't. Are you? Will you receive a rich welcome into heaven? I would rather you face this question this side of eternity than the other.

Who Will Go To Heaven?

My four year old son Luke has asked me on two or three occasions whether he is a Christian. How would you answer him? Most conversations on this subject go something like this:

> Luke: "Daddy, am I a Christian?"
> Dad: "Well, what do you have to do to become a Christian?"
> Luke: "Repent and trust in Jesus Christ."
> Dad: "Well, have you repented and trusted in Jesus Christ?"
> Luke: "Yes!"

Dad: "Well, then you're a Christian."

Sadly, because I have mistaken Luke's question of "How do I *know* I am a Christian?" for "How do I *become* a Christian?" I have answered the second question but not the first. The question of how one becomes a Christian is different from how one knows they are a Christian.[1] Otherwise why did the apostle John—who wrote to assure people of their salvation (1 John 5:13)—not just remind us how to become a Christian?

I was surfing the internet and came across a chat room where this question—"How do I know I am a Christian?"—was being discussed. One person said that only those "who obey God" go "to heaven." Another claimed that God "cares about how we feel in our hearts toward Him" and what counts is "if he has accepted Jesus in his heart, and there are some Christians that might not make it, that is God's [sic] choice, for only he knows our hearts." Another said that "salvation is about faith in Jesus Christ as Lord and savior. That means a personal relationship with Jesus Christ. With salvation comes assurance of going to heaven." One person suggested that Catholics "might be more likely to get to heaven" since a Catholic attends "confession . . . and confesses all his sins and is absolved of them by the priest." Finally someone said that "Catholics, Protestants, Baptists, Mormons, Presbyterians, 7th Day Adventists, etc., all consider Jesus to be the messiah, so all are Christians."

What Does The Bible Say?

It may seem an odd question at first: "Who will go to heaven?" Isn't the answer obvious? Do not an overwhelming number of Bible passages speak of salvation by grace through faith in Jesus Christ? "For it is by grace you have been saved, through faith—and this

---

1. Will Metzger, *Tell The Truth: The Whole Gospel to the Whole Person by Whole People,* revised edition (Downers Grove: IVP, 2002), 79.

is not from yourselves, it is the gift of God—not by works, so that no one can boast" (Eph. 2:8–9; see also Rom. 3:24, 28; 4:1–5; 5:1; 10:10; Gal. 2:16; 3:11, 24; Phil. 3:9).

Works are not just secondary to salvation, they are excluded altogether. We who have been saved have been so "not because of anything we have done but because of his own purpose and grace" (2 Tim. 1:9). Our salvation is "not because of righteous things we had done, but because of his mercy. He saved us through the washing of rebirth and renewal by the Holy Spirit" (Titus 3:5). This is all clear.

According to Paul and Silas

In Acts 16 we find Paul and Silas in prison when there is a great earthquake and the prison doors fly open and the prisoners' chains fall off. The distraught prison warden pleads with Paul and Silas, "What must I do to be saved?" Does he mean salvation from harm or hell? It doesn't matter, but what is important is Paul and Silas' response: "Believe in the Lord Jesus, and you will be saved—you and your household" (Acts 16:31).

FIGURE 1: SALVATION: ONE ANSWER

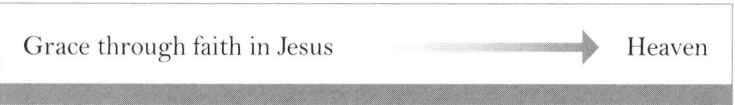

According to Jesus

Is this all the Bible has to say about how we are saved? Do these passages, and similar ones, present the *complete* doctrine of salvation?

Is there another side to it? Consider two examples from Jesus' teaching.

> On one occasion an expert in the law stood up to test Jesus. "Teacher," he asked, "What must I do to inherit eternal life?" "What is written in the Law?" he replied. "How do you read it?" He answered: "'Love the Lord your God with all your heart and with all your soul and with all your strength and with all your mind'; and, 'Love your neighbor as yourself.'" "You have answered correctly," Jesus replied. "*Do this and you will live*" (Luke 10:25–28).

According to Jesus, to inherit eternal life one must "love God!" Admittedly love is not belief, but surely belief includes love (see John 8:42; 16:27; James 2:5; 1 Pet. 1:8). It is the second part of the lawyer's reply, however, that is unsettling—"Love your neighbor as yourself." What's more, Jesus affirms the lawyer's answer and tells him, "*Do* this and you will live." Thus, if you do not love your neighbor you will not live (eternally). Let's consider another example:

> Now a man came up to Jesus and asked, "Teacher, what good thing must I do to get eternal life?" . . . Jesus replied . . . "*If you want to enter life,* obey the commandments." "Which ones?" the man inquired. Jesus replied, "'Do not murder, do not commit adultery, do not steal, do not give false testimony, honor your father and mother,' and 'love your neighbor as yourself.'" "All these I have kept," the young man said. "What do I still lack?" Jesus answered, "*If you want to be perfect,* go, sell your possessions and give to the poor, and you will have treasure in heaven" (Matt .19:16–21).

Here Jesus' response is even more disturbing. If this rich man wants to get eternal life, he must obey the commandments. This is clear. So much so that one scholar writes, "There is a relationship between eternal life and keeping the commandments."[2] If that is not disturbing enough, Jesus then asks this man to sell all his possessions in order to be perfect and have treasure in heaven.

Hence there seem to be two strands of teaching on the subject of salvation; two answers we might even say.

FIGURE 2: SALVATION: ANOTHER ANSWER

Do / Obey → Heaven

Now for those who are committed to the notion that the Bible is inspired and is without error, part of which means that it does not contradict itself, the idea that the Bible presents two differing answers to such an important question is intolerable. And for good reason. The process of inspiration leaves no room for God contradicting himself or being confused on any issue (2 Tim. 3:16; 2 Pet. 1:21). We must assume, therefore, that even though there appear to be two answers, there is in fact only one, and the two answers are not contradictory but complementary.

Works Do Influence Where We Spend Eternity

The answers given to the lawyer and the rich man are a long way from the answer Paul and Silas gave to the jailor at Philippi. Paul says, "Believe!" and Jesus says, "Do!" If the lawyer and the rich man were but two isolated examples, we could perhaps console ourselves

---

2. Jeannine K. Brown, *The Disciples in Narrative Perspective: The Portrayal and Function of the Matthean Disciples*, Academia Biblica, ed. Saul M. Olyan and Mark Allan Powell, no. 9 (Atlanta: SBL, 2002), 81–82.

with some alternative interpretations. These examples, however, are not isolated, for Jesus' teaching is replete with similar instruction on what people must do to receive eternal life. Here is a mere *sampling* of some of the more obvious passages:

> For I tell you that unless your righteousness surpasses that of the Pharisees and the teachers of the law, you will certainly not enter the kingdom of heaven (Matt. 5:20).
>
> I tell you that anyone who is angry with his brother will be subject to judgment . . . anyone who says, 'You fool!' will be in danger of the fire of hell (Matt. 5:22).
>
> Not everyone who says to me, "Lord, Lord," will enter the kingdom of heaven, but only he who does the will of my Father who is in heaven (Matt. 7:21).
>
> He who stands firm to the end will be saved (Matt. 10:22; see also Matt. 24:9; Mark 13:13; Luke 21:19).
>
> Then the King will say to those on his right, "Come, you who are blessed by my Father; take your inheritance, the kingdom prepared for you since the creation of the world. For I was hungry and you gave me something to eat, I was thirsty and you gave me something to drink, I was a stranger and you invited me in, I needed clothes and you clothed me, I was sick and you looked after me, I was in prison and you came to visit me" . . . . Then he will say to those on his left, "Depart from me, you who are cursed, into the eternal fire prepared for the devil and his angels. For I was hungry and you gave me nothing to eat. . . . Then they will go away to eternal punishment, but the righteous to eternal life (Matt. 25:34–36, 41–42, 46).

Concerning this last passage one New Testament scholar writes, "[Jesus] provides an interesting criterion for those who will be judged . . . an interesting theological problem arises as to how such a criterion accords with the doctrine of salvation by grace, *since here salvation seems to depend on works.*"³

There are other passages less explicit but no less disturbing:

> For if you forgive men when they sin against you, your heavenly Father will also forgive you. But if you do not forgive men their sins, your Father will not forgive your sins (Matt. 6:14–15; see also Mark 11:25).
>
> Do not judge, or you too will be judged (Matt. 7:1; see also Luke 6:37).
>
> Whoever acknowledges me before men, I will also acknowledge him before my Father in heaven. But whoever disowns me before men, I will disown him before my Father in heaven (Matt. 10:32–33; see also Luke 12:8–9).
>
> I tell you that men will have to give account on the day of judgment for every careless word they have spoken. For by your words you will be acquitted, and by your words you will be condemned (Matt. 12:36–37).
>
> "You wicked servant," he said, "I canceled all that debt of yours because you begged me to. Shouldn't you have had mercy on your fellow servant just as I had on you?" In anger his master turned him over to the jailers to be tortured, until he should pay back all he owed. This is how my heavenly Father will treat each of you unless you forgive your brother from your heart (Matt. 18:32–35).

It is not surprising that another well known New Testament scholar has suggested that Jesus' "emphasis on obedience may lead one to think that good works are necessary to merit entrance into

---

3. Kristen Stendahl, *Paul among Jews and Gentiles: And Other Essays* (Philadelphia: Fortress, 1963), 62–63 (emphasis mine).

the kingdom."[4] It is for this reason that the late John Gerstner wrote, "Christ repeatedly makes good works a *condition* for salvation."[5] Can we conclude anything else? Jesus' words plainly state it, scholars agree with it: *The presence or absence of works influences where we will spend eternity.*

A Serious Message

I can think of no more important topic than salvation and eternity. These matters are not merely for the theologically educated or those Christians with a keen bent towards the "deeper things" of the Word. The very fact that God has given us his Word in the form that he has suggests that he wants us *all* to think about these passages. I can think of three reasons why this subject is seriously important.

The Reality of False Converts

There are at least three *clear* examples in the New Testament of false conversions; instances where people believed in Jesus and yet did not receive salvation.

Some Wanted Miracles

The first involves "many people [who] saw the miraculous signs [Jesus] was doing and believed in his name" (John 2:23). At first glance we would expect these people to be saved. After all, John 3:18 clearly states, "Whoever believes in him is not condemned, but whoever does not believe stands condemned already because he has not *believed in the name* of God's one and only Son." And yet in

---

4. Thomas R. Schreiner, *The Law and Its Fulfillment: A Pauline Theology of Law* (Grand Rapids: Baker, 1993), 209.
5. John H. Gerstner, *Wrongly Dividing the Word of Truth: A Critique of Dispensationalism*, ed. Don Kistler, 2d ed. (Morgan, PA: Soli Deo Gloria, 2000), 299.

spite of this "Jesus would not entrust himself to them" (John 2:24a). That's odd! These people believed in *his name*. However, we are given the explanation as to why Jesus would not entrust himself to them: "*for* he knew all men. He did not need man's testimony about man, for he knew what was in a man" (John 2:24b–25). Evidently, then, salvation is more than just saying the words "I believe." They must come from the heart. In fact, the heart is central as Romans 10:9–10 points out:

> If you confess with your mouth, "Jesus is Lord,"
> And believe in your *heart* that God raised him from the dead,
>   you will be saved.
> For it is with your *heart* that you believe and are justified,
> And it is with your mouth that you confess and are saved.

The way Paul has structured these verses is significant. Mouth confession is important, but the crux—note that *heart* appears twice in the centre of this passage—is belief with the heart. Saying the words, even words from the Bible, is not enough. It must come from the heart. These people described in John 2:23 merely wanted a miracle worker.

Some Wanted a License to Sin

On one occasion while Jesus was speaking "many put their faith in him" (John 8:30). Jesus then addresses some of the Jews "who had believed him" (John 8:31a)[6] who claimed that God was their Father

---

6. The Greek construction between John 8:30 and v. 31 is different. Verse 30: "many put their *faith in him* (*episteusan eis auton*)"; v. 31: "To the Jews who had *believed him* (*pepisteukotas autô*)." Because the constructions are different some have suggested that v. 30 refers to genuine saving faith while v. 31 refers to false faith and a different group of people. However, in John's Gospel the same Greek constructions can be used for true faith and false faith. For example, in John 2:23 the same Greek construction occurs as in 8:30 and refers to false faith. In John 5:24 the same Greek construction occurs as in John 8:31 and refers to genuine faith. I should also point out that the English words "faith" and "believe" are the same Greek word—*pisteuô*.

(John 8:41). However, their faith means nothing to Jesus since they do not hold to his teaching (John 8:31b). They have no room for his word (John 8:37). They do not live like Abraham lived (John 8:39). They are therefore still slaves to sin (John 8:34). God is not their Father at all; Satan is (John 8:44).

Jude described such people as "godless men, who change the grace of our God into a license for immorality and deny Jesus Christ our only Sovereign and Lord" (Jude 4). They certainly do not live like Christians (see Jude 8, 10, 13, 16, 19) in spite of the fact that they attend church (Jude 12). Yet they "do not have the Spirit" (Jude 19). Consequently, "blackest darkness has been reserved forever" for them (Jude 13).

Some Wanted Personal Gain

While Philip was preaching the good news of Jesus Christ a magician named Simon "believed and was baptized. He then followed Philip everywhere, astonished by the great signs and miracles he saw" (Acts 8:13). There was no reason at this point to suspect Simon's conversion is less than genuine except that he appeared especially enamored with Philip's miracles (cf. John 2:23).

Peter and John then turned up and laid hands on those who had believed "and they received the Holy Spirit" (Acts 8:17). When Simon saw this, "he offered them money and said, 'Give me also this ability so that everyone on whom I lay my hands may receive the Holy Spirit'" (Acts 8:18–19). Simon sees this as an opportunity to advance his fame beyond that of a mere magician. Peter however puts a stop to it and says, "May your money perish with you, because you thought you could buy the gift of God with money! You have no part or share in this ministry, because your heart is not right before God. Repent of this wickedness and pray to the Lord. Perhaps he will forgive you for having such a thought in your heart. For I see that you are full of bitterness and captive to sin" (Acts 8:20–23).

Several factors suggest that Simon's conversion is false; I will mention two.[7] First, Simon will "perish" unless he repents. The term "perish" *always* means eternal destruction (Matt. 7:13; Rom. 9:22; Heb. 10:39; Rev. 17:8, 11; cf. also 2 Pet. 3:7). Second, when repentance is called for in Acts it is *always* for salvation (Acts 2:38; 3:19; 5:31; 11:18; 17:30; 20:21; 26:20).

Sober Warnings

These three examples provide us with some sober warnings. First, one may believe in Jesus Christ and remain unsaved. "Not everyone who says to me, 'Lord, Lord,' will enter the kingdom of heaven" (Matt. 7:21a). Not everyone who prays the prayer, walks the aisle, goes to church, sings the songs and so on will be saved but "only he who does the will of my Father who is in heaven" (Matt. 7:21b). This means that for some salvation is simply an "appearance" (Luke 8:13). They have believed a "different gospel" and "a Jesus other than the Jesus" in the New Testament (2 Cor. 11:4). They have believed but received God's grace in "vain" (1 Cor. 15:2; 2 Cor. 6:1). Sadly, they have indeed deceived themselves (James 1:16).

A hope of acceptance by God based on such things as going forward in a meeting, praying a suggested prayer, imitating

---

7. Many other points suggest that Simon's conversion at this point is false. First, Peter tells Simon, "You have no part or share in this ministry." The word "share" occurs in Acts 26:18 to describe those who have turned "from the power of Satan to God, so that they may receive forgiveness of sins and a *place* [share] among those who are sanctified by faith in me." Second, Peter tells Simon, "Your heart is not right before God." In Acts whenever anything negative is said of the heart, the person(s) is an unbeliever (Acts 5:3–4; 7:39, 51, 54; 28:27). Conversely, positive statements refer to believers (Acts 2:46; 4:32; 15:9; 16:14). Third, Peter suggests that God might "forgive" Simon. Forgiveness in Acts *is always* related to salvation (Acts 2:38; 5:31; 10:43; 13:38; 26:18). Fourth, Simon is said to be "full of bitterness and captive to sin." The NIV has translated the Greek phrase *bond of unrighteousness* as "captive to sin." In Luke-Acts the unrighteous are unbelievers (Luke 13:27; 18:6, 11; Acts 1:18; 24:15).

the experience of others, joining a church, attending many Christian meetings, being baptized, studying the Bible regularly, helping others, feeling good in a religious service or having a strong conviction that they are right with God is a hope not found on biblical truths . . . people can be involved in any or all of these activities without ever looking to Jesus Christ as the only Savior and Lord. Without this there is no salvation. Without this there is no assurance.[8]

Second, becoming a Christian is not a ticket to heaven or a license to sin. The apostle Paul addressed this very issue when he asked, "Shall we sin because we are not under law but under grace?" (Rom. 6:15). Of course not, he says, and the reason is "that you have been set free from sin and have become slaves to God, the benefit you reap leads to holiness, and the result is eternal life. For the wages of sin is death" (Rom. 6:22–23). Those who want to continue in a life of sin because they are "saved by grace" will receive the wages of sin.[9]

Third, becoming a Christian is not about receiving Jesus for what he can do for us. The so-called prosperity gospel teaches that God promises to make us healthy and prosperous. This is, however, a gross misrepresentation of what God promises. The Bible promises that those who belong to God's kingdom will be persecuted (Matt. 5:10; 2 Tim. 3:12; 1 Pet. 4:12). Their life will not be easy (Matt. 7:13–14) nor will they be popular (John 15:18–19).

A young lady approached me some time ago and wanted some advice on what to say to a Christian friend who believed—because of what her pastor preached as part of the gospel—that God wanted her to be healthy and wealthy. At that point I explained that such a

---

8. Metzger, *Tell The Truth*, 80.
9. That eternal or spiritual death is in view here is evident since Paul goes on to say, "the gift of God is eternal life" (Rom 6:23b).

gospel would save no one. People are not to come to God for what they can get. They are to come to him for who he is.[10]

Imagine that you were exceedingly wealthy and someone befriended you because of your wealth. Consequently, they visited you a lot, had you over for meals, and in general did everything anyone would do to build a close relationship with you. However, all this time their hope was—unbeknown to you—that you would offload some of your wealth on to them. How would you feel if you knew that the motivation behind their friendship with you was money? I would imagine you'd feel hurt. No one likes to be wanted for any other reason except that they themselves are worth wanting. God is no different. He is not a means to an end; he is the end. "He can't be used as a road," C. S. wrote. "If you're approaching Him not as the goal but as a road, not as the end but as the means, you're not really approaching Him at all."[11]

The Error of "Once Saved Always Saved"

The second reason why this subject is important is to caution us against using what has become a misused cliché within Christendom, "once saved, always saved." The intent of this phrase is to convey the idea that once a person becomes a Christian they are always a Christian and can never lose their salvation. The problem, though, is not so much in the message this phrase conveys—I believe that the message is fundamentally correct. The problem is in the way the hearer understands it. I may say to someone that once they are saved, they are always saved. However, they might hear me as saying, "Once I have *believed*, I am always saved." But this is not what I said!

How this cliché can affect the way we live was brought home to me years ago when I was talking with a guy who professed to be a

---

10. I highly recommend John Piper, *God is the Gospel: Meditations on God's Love as the Gift of Himself* (Wheaton: Crossway, 2005).
11. C. S. Lewis, *A Grief Observed* (New York: Bantam, 1976), 79.

Christian and was at one time heavily involved in our youth group, though he was now not living as a Christian in any sense whatsoever. He told me that he knew he was okay because of his "conversion." He knew, he said, what he had to do, and that one day, when the time was right, he would return to the Lord. How deceived he was because he had been brought up believing, "once saved, always saved."

Properly understanding this phrase is a declaration of God's faithfulness towards those he saves. It is not a promise to all who say, "I believe in Jesus." We have already seen that someone can say, "I believe" and still not be saved. The Pharisees *claimed* they could see spiritually, yet Jesus told them they were guilty because they were still blind (John 9:41). Paul knew of people who *claimed* "to know God, but by their actions they deny him" (Titus 1:16). James states that the mere *claim* to have faith not supported by deeds is of no value concerning salvation (James 2:14). Even the demons have that kind of faith (James 2:18). We can make all sorts of claims regarding our relationship with God but claims are cheap without proof. "If we *claim* to have fellowship with him yet walk in the darkness, we lie and do not live by the truth" (1 John 1:6).

Eternal Destinies Are At Stake

How incredibly sad that people are going to hell, not because they don't realize it—though that is sad enough—but because they are actually doing, or have done, what they believe will save them from hell. That has to be the ultimate deception, the ultimate tragedy. Picture these people standing before Jesus saying to him, "Lord, Lord, did we not prophesy in your name, and in your name drive out demons and perform many miracles?" (Matt. 7:22) only to have Jesus look them in the eye and say, "I *never* knew you" (Matt. 7:23). Can you imagine their utter disbelief? "You what! You never knew me? How can that possibly be? I believed; I was even baptized (Acts 8:13). I attended church regularly (Jude 12). I had faith (James

2:14). God is my Father (John 8:41). I'm an heir of Abraham (John 8:39). I'm a Christian" (John 9:41). How terribly sad. Unbelievers at least will surely not be surprised to hear of their destiny, but "believers" surely will be. How tragic!

An Unpopular Message

I am under no delusions that this message will be popular. To question something so near and dear is a taboo subject. "Aren't I meant to have assurance? Isn't it wrong to doubt? Am I not doubting the sure promises of God in his Word? Surely I can't go through life wondering if I'm saved? I've always been told it's wrong to question. Questioning my salvation makes me feel uncomfortable."

We might well ask then, "Is it kind to shatter a person's hope of salvation?"

The answer is, "Yes, because without scriptural grounds, it is nothing more than a false hope."[12] False hopes won't admit anybody into heaven regardless of how earnest they might be. Esau "sought the blessing with tears" but to no avail (Heb. 12:17).

As a teacher and a pastor I want people, myself included, to feel the full brunt of the warnings of Scripture. In kindness I want to alert people to the fact that Christ will say to some, "I never knew you. Away from me, you evildoers!" (Matt. 7:23). I want them to know that they cannot just crawl under a "once saved, always saved" sign and let the message pass them by. It's kind to tell people this side of heaven rather than letting them discover it for themselves when it's too late—all because we don't want them to feel threatened.

Let's learn from history. The majority of God's people seem to have tenaciously refused to listen to God's prophets, and they have done so to their peril. Beginning nine or so centuries before

---

12. Metzger, *Tell The Truth*, 80.

Christ, king Ahab of Israel hated listening to one particular prophet "because he never prophesies anything good about me, but always bad" (1 Kings 22:8). Isaiah brought a message of judgment, but the people wanted "no more visions of what is right! Tell us pleasant things, prophesy illusions," they said (Isa. 30:10). They would have rather put up with liars and deceivers "prophesy[ing] . . . plenty of wine and beer" than hear the penetrating truth (Mic. 2:11). Jeremiah preached judgment, and what was the response? "You must die!" (Jer. 26:8). Assurance and peace is what they wanted, not warning (Jer. 5:31; Ezek. 13:10).

One would think they would have treated Jesus better, but they didn't. Even those who knew him best "took offense at him" (Mark 6:3). The Pharisees didn't like being preached to. Jesus' teaching threatened their security, so they eventually killed him. The apostle Paul had to warn his readers about certain people whose preaching was smooth and flattering, yet "they deceive the minds of naive people" (Rom. 16:18). He reminds young Timothy, "The time will come when men will not put up with sound doctrine. Instead, to suit their own desires, they will gather around them a great number of teachers to say what their itching ears want to hear" (2 Tim. 4:3).

This is a disturbing trend. Genuine believers will not feel threatened by warnings. They will welcome them. We need to take care that we do not merely want our ears tickled.

A Kind Message

We also need to realize that this message is not intended to take anything away from us. January 1987 was when I decided to give myself to God. I had been going to church and reading the Bible for about two months. The moment I decided that I wanted to "commit," though, I was nowhere near a Bible or a church. I was actually on our family farm in New Zealand. I prayed and asked God to take control of my life. I thought nothing of sin or Jesus or even heaven or hell. For at least eight years following, I often doubted whether I really did "get saved" that day. I somehow felt that if it did not happen on *that day* then I was lost.

I believe that many Christians look back to their time of "decision" for assurance as if salvation *had* to take place *that day*. If something or someone casts doubt on their past moment of salvation, they feel threatened as though nothing can be done about it now. It happened (or didn't) in the past and they can't change it. We don't like thinking that the past ten, twenty, or however many years since our "decision" may have actually been lost, our soul with them!

There's no need to be defensive or feel threatened. I write this book for the *good* of everyone who reads it, not to threaten anyone. I write it in the hope that souls might be genuinely saved "so that you will receive what [God] has promised" (Heb. 10:36). I write in kindness to alert you to what Christ will say to some—perhaps you—unless you take heed on the day of judgment: "Not everyone who says to me, 'Lord, Lord,' will enter the kingdom of heaven" (Matt. 7:21).

CHAPTER TWO

GRACE AND WORKS: ARE THEY OPPOSED?

To sum things up: First, there is more to salvation than making a decision. There are many examples of false professions in the Bible, and we should not think that there would be any less in our churches today. Second, works *do* influence where we spend eternity. This might disturb you—if it were not for the fact that Jesus taught it! Of course, you may still be disturbed, but I hope it's not because you doubt what the Scriptures so plainly say. The church through the ages understood these realities.

The well-known fourth century church father, Augustine—dubbed the Doctor of *Grace,* by the way—declared that "eternal life is given in return for good works."[1] Martin Luther, the renowned reformer to whom we are so thankful for his insistence on justification by grace alone through faith alone, even stated, "Works are necessary to salvation, but they do not cause salvation, because faith alone gives life. On account of the hypocrisy we must say that good works

---

1. Augustine, *Grace and Free Will* 8.19 (in *The Fathers of the Church: A New Translation*, ed. Joseph Deferrari, vol. 59 [Washington, DC: The Catholic University of America Press, 1968]).

are necessary to salvation."[2] Luther's successor John Calvin suggested that God leads his people into possession of eternal life "by the course of good works."[3] Later John Wesley taught that holiness is the "ordinary, stated condition of final justification."[4] Eighteen hundred years of church history[5] supports the notion that works influence where we spend eternity.

But how does this square with salvation by grace through faith apart from works? It is important that we take some time to answer this question. Once we know the answer, the "difficult" passages that so plainly speak to this issue will make a lot more sense.

The Danger of Not Defining Terms

Have you ever been speaking with someone about a particular subject only to discover that what you meant was not what they meant? Having lived outside of my homeland, New Zealand, for nearly fifteen years, I know only too well this experience. I remember in seminary asking someone for a "rubber." I wanted to rub out, or erase, a word I had written in pencil. A "rubber" in the American mind, however, is a condom. How embarrassing! It is important to define our terms. We need to be clear that we are talking about the same thing.

---

2. Martin Luther, *Luther's Works*, vol. 34, ed. Helmut T. Lehmann (Philadelphia: Muhlenberg Press, 1955), 165.
3. John Calvin, *Institutes of the Christian Religion,* trans. Henry Beveridge, vol. 2 (Grand Rapids: Eerdmans, 1975), 3.18.1.
4. John Wesley, *The Works of John Wesley,* 1st ed., vol. 8 (London: Wesleyan Conference, 1872; reprint, Grand Rapids: Zondervan, 1958), 56.
5. I have written more extensively on the relationship between works and salvation in church history in Alan P. Stanley, *Did Jesus Teach Salvation By Works: The Role of Works in Salvation in the Synoptic Gospels,* The Evangelical Theological Society Monograph Series, ed. David W. Baker, vol. 4 (Eugene, OR: Pickwick, 2006), 19–70.

WHY EMPHASIZE WORKS?

Salvation is by grace. God's gracious intervention does not merely entail bringing us into a relationship with him and letting us bide our time until heaven, however. Jesus chose us "to go and bear fruit—fruit that will last" (John 15:16). Fruit bearing is not optional, for "every tree that does not produce good fruit will be cut down and thrown into the fire" (Matt. 3:10; 7:19).

A superficial—or even deep and joyful—confession will not save anyone (Matt. 13:20–21). We may call Jesus "Lord, Lord," all we like, but unless we do the will of his Father we will not enter the kingdom of heaven (Matt. 7:21). Doing God's will is what counts. Thus, "you need to persevere so that when you have done the *will of God,* you will receive what he has promised" (Heb. 10:36). It is only "the man who does the *will of God* [who] lives forever" (1 John 2:17).

We may have an impressive spiritual record—"Did we not prophesy in your name and in your name drive out demons and perform many miracles?" (Matt. 7:22) But if we do not know Jesus, we will be excluded from his presence for all eternity (Matt. 7:23; cf. John 17:3).

We may be very religious and think of ourselves as quite obedient. We may attend church regularly and read the Bible meticulously. We might describe ourselves as "good" people. But "unless your righteousness surpasses that of the Pharisees and the teachers of the law, you will certainly not enter the kingdom of heaven" (Matt. 5:20).

Listen to what Paul says to those who live their lives practicing "sexual immorality, impurity and debauchery; idolatry and witchcraft; hatred, discord, jealousy, fits of rage, selfish ambition, dissensions, factions and envy; drunkenness, orgies, and the like. I warn you, as I did before, that those who live like this will not inherit the kingdom of God" (Gal. 5:19–21). "For of this you can be sure: No immoral, impure or greedy person—such a man is an idolater—has any inheritance in the kingdom of Christ and of God" (Eph. 5:5).

But still you ask, "How is it that we are saved by grace through faith, yet we must produce fruit to be saved?" There are at least four reasons why, as John Calvin said, "eternal life [is] a consequence of works."[6] I will look at the first two reasons in this chapter and the second two in the next.

Two Kinds of Works

The *first* clue as to why fruit/works play a role in salvation is to understand that there are two kinds of works. Man-made works are abhorrent to salvation, whereas God-produced works are indispensable.

Man-made Works

If it was up to us we would probably praise many of the works that Jesus condemns and condemn many of the works he praises. We know that murder, adultery, theft and the like are wrong; these works are always ungodly (e.g., Mark 7:20–23). But there are others: prophesying, casting out demons and doing miracles, even in Jesus' name, will sometimes turn out to be evil (Matt. 7:21–23). What makes these works "evil"[7] is that they have not been done according to the Father's will (Matt. 7:21). They are what we might call "fleshly."

The religious leaders also carry out what might appear to be godly works. They wear reminders for prayer on their arms (called *phylacteries*), take visible seats at worship centers, and greet people in the market places. Yet Jesus warns the crowds to "not do according to their w*orks*" (Matt. 23:3, my translation). It's not the works that

---

6. Calvin, *Institutes,* 3.14.21.
7. The NIV has translated the Greek "workers of lawlessness" into "evildoers."

are evil but the motivation behind them: they "are done for men to see" (Matt. 23:5).

Giving, praying, and fasting are surely commendable works (Matt. 6:1–18). But once again Jesus looks to the motivation behind them. In this case people are motivated by a desire to please people. They are "hypocrites" (Matt. 6:2, 5, 16). This is serious, for hypocrites do not enter the kingdom (Matt. 23:13). Rather they are going to hell (Matt. 23:15) where there will be "weeping and gnashing of teeth" (Matt. 24:51).

God-Produced Works

On the other hand there are works that might appear to be worthy of condemnation but are in fact praised by Jesus. The woman who poured expensive perfume on Jesus' head is ridiculed by the disciples because she has wasted valuable perfume. Yet in Jesus' assessment, "she has done a good work" (Matt. 26:10, my translation). Once again the heart is key.

"Good *deeds*" (Greek = "works") can be instrumental in leading people to God (Matt. 5:16). Such works originate with God, for "whoever lives by the truth comes into the light, so that it may be seen plainly that what he has done (Greek = "works") has been done *through God*" (John 3:21, parenthesis mine). Similarly, Jesus says in John 14:12: "I tell you the truth, anyone who has faith in me will do *works* that I do." Just what these works are need not concern us here. The point is that they cannot occur apart from faith in Jesus.

It is this new relationship between Jesus and his disciples that makes godly "works" possible. For this reason Jesus tells his disciples that the only way to produce fruit is to remain in him (John 15:1–4). Bearing fruit does not and cannot happen apart from being connected to Jesus. Thus Jesus says, "Apart from me you can do nothing" (John 15:5).

Works Outside of the Gospels[8]

In the book of Acts those who turn to the Lord confess "their evil *deeds*" (Acts 19:18), and having done so, they must then "prove their repentance by their *deeds*" (Acts 26:20).

Paul declares that we are saved "not by *works*, so that no one can boast" (Eph. 2:9). What he means is that we are not saved by *our* works—"this not from yourselves" (Eph. 2:8). But there is a place for works. "For we are God's workmanship, created in Christ Jesus to do good *works*, which God prepared in advance for us to do" (Eph. 2:10). Clearly these are Christian works and thus only possible for those who are a new creation ("created in Christ Jesus"). For "Jesus Christ . . . gave himself for us to redeem us from all wickedness and to purify for himself a people that are his very own, eager for good *works*" (Titus 2:14, my translation).

According to Hebrews there are "*works* that lead to death" (Heb. 6:1, my translation) until one experiences the cleansing blood of Christ (Heb. 9:14). Once cleansed, Christians are to "spur one another on toward . . . good *deeds*" (Heb. 10:24). These works "accompany salvation" (Heb. 6:9–10) and are produced only by God who "equip[s] you with everything good for doing his will" (Heb. 13:21).

James warns his readers that genuine faith must be accompanied by "deeds" (James 2:14; cf. 3:13). Christians will be "pure; then peace-loving, considerate, submissive, full of mercy and good fruit, impartial and sincere" (James 3:17–18). Those controlled by the devil, however, will be characterized by "envy and selfish ambition. . . disorder and every evil practice" (James 3:14–16).

Peter encourages "good deeds" among his Christian readers because unbelievers may see them and "glorify God on the day he

---

8. For more on works in the New Testament see Stanley, *Did Jesus Teach Salvation By Works*, 116–33.

visits us" (1 Pet. 2:12). Christians, however, will be repulsed by the "lawless deeds" that characterize the ungodly (2 Pet. 2:8).

In the book of Revelation there are "deeds" that include "love and faith . . . service and perseverance" (Rev. 2:19). These are strictly Christian. However there are also "deeds" performed by the unrepentant—"worshiping demons, and idols of gold, silver, bronze, stone and wood" (Rev. 9:20).

FIGURE 3: WORKS

Pre-Christian works originating from yourselves	✝	Christian works only possible in Christ

SUMMARY

The existence of two kinds of works in the New Testament is our first clue to understanding why Jesus will not admit everyone who calls him "Lord, Lord," into his kingdom. Evil or lawless works—works that originate from ourselves—play no role in our salvation. They are fleshly and originate from the devil, providing a means for boasting in our own accomplishments. For this reason God "saved us, not because of righteous works *we* had done" (Titus 3:5).

Clearly, works are important. The rich young ruler was to sell all he had. The lawyer is to love his neighbor. We must stand firm until the end. Our righteousness must surpass that of the Pharisees and the teachers of the law. We must do the Father's will. These "works" cannot originate from ourselves. They must originate with God, and they can only do so in the lives of Christians. These are the works Martin Luther had in mind when he said that "works are necessary to salvation" and when John Calvin said that God leads his people into possession of eternal life "by the course of good works."

Two Kinds of Grace

The second reason that fruit is inevitable and necessary among those who are saved has to do with grace. The question is sometimes asked, "But aren't grace and works opposed?" Well, there is more to grace than we normally think.

Grace is God's Undeserved Favor

Grace is often described as an acronym: "God's Riches At Christ's Expense." Salvation does not originate with ourselves; it is a generous and undeserved gift (see Eph. 2:8–9; Titus 3:5, 7). Our redemption is "by grace, then it is no longer by works; if it were, grace would no longer be grace" (Rom. 11:6). Works merely provide an opportunity for boasting in self.

We human beings are a strange lot. If God asked us to run up and down a mountain six times, jog on the spot for an hour, pioneer our way through a leech-infested jungle, and finish with one hundred pushups to put us in good stead with him, many of us would probably do it, or at least try. I would! And yet when God asks us to accept the free offer of righteousness through his Son, many of us turn him down as if to say, "Where's the boasting in that?" Grace provides an opportunity for boasting in God.

In light of what we have just learned concerning works, we need to keep in mind that the above passages—Ephesians 2:8–9; Titus 3:5, 7; Romans 11:6—all concern pre-Christian works. *Pre-Christian works* stand opposed to grace because they are produced by human effort. This is not so with *Christian works*.

Grace is Power in Us

The standard Greek lexicon says that grace, in certain passages, is "to be understood in a very concrete sense."[9] It is virtually synonymous with "power." Thus, "Stephen, a man full of God's grace and power, did great wonders and miraculous signs among the people" (Acts. 6:8). God's grace provided Paul with power in his suffering (2 Cor. 12:9).

What is remarkable is that this "incomparably great power" is within every Christian (Eph. 1:19). It is there because God himself lives inside every believer (Phil. 2:13) through his Spirit (Gal. 5:16, 22–25; 2 Thess. 2:13). But even more remarkable is the nature of this power. "That power is like the working of [God's] mighty strength, which he exerted in Christ when he raised him from the dead and seated him at his right hand in the heavenly realms" (Eph. 1:19–20). Imagine that! The same power that raised Christ from the dead dwells inside every Christian (see also Rom. 8:11; Col. 2:12; cf. 2 Pet. 1:3). All the energy in the entire world could not bring a dead person back to life. And yet Christians have the very power that raised Christ from the dead within them. Incredible! This same power will eventually transform our earthly bodies into something akin to Christ's glorious body when he returns (Phil. 3:21). Even now, this power is working within every Christian. Thus understood, grace achieves a number of things:

1. *Grace affects us*—Paul claimed that God's "grace to me was not without effect. No, I worked harder than all of them— yet not I, but the *grace* of God that was with me" (1 Cor. 15:10). God's grace had an effect in his life, and the effect was hard work. It is the entire New Testament's assumption that grace is not without effect in any believer's life.

2. *Grace changes us*—"The grace of God that brings salvation

---

9. Walter Bauer, William F. Arndt and F. Wilbur Gingrich, *A Greek-English Lexicon of the New Testament and Other Early Christian Literature*, 3rd ed., rev. Frederick William Danker (Chicago: University of Chicago Press, 2000), 1080.

has appeared to all men. It [grace] teaches us to say 'no' to ungodliness and worldly passions, and to live self-controlled, upright and godly lives in this present age" (Titus 2:11–12). Notice what grace does: it changes us. It produces "self-controlled, upright and godly lives in this present age." We are changed when we get to heaven, but change begins here. It changes us into the people God wants us to be and enables us to serve others (1 Pet. 4:17; cf. Rom. 12:6; Eph. 4:7).

3. *Grace testifies to our salvation*—Grace then, or at least its effects and changes, can be seen. James, Peter and John "recognized the grace given to" Paul (Gal. 2:9). Upon meeting the new Christians at Antioch, Barnabas "saw the evidence of the grace of God" (Acts 11:23). Grace had produced something; there were changes and effects—the testimony of God's grace at work in believers.

Grace-Produced Works

It is this understanding of grace that provides the second clue as to why fruit is necessary in salvation. Grace produces this fruit. In other words, this fruit is a gift! This is such a crucial point to grasp. The entry requirements for the kingdom—doing God's will and surpassing righteousness and so on—can only be produced by God's enabling grace. In response to the question, How is eternal life both a reward for service and a free gift of grace? Augustine answered:

> This question, then, seems to me to be by no means capable of solution, unless we understand that even those good works of ours, which are recompensed with eternal life, belong to the grace of God, because of what is said by the Lord Jesus: "Without me ye can do nothing." . . . It follows, then, dearly beloved, beyond all doubt, that as your good life is nothing else than God's grace, so also the eternal life which is the

recompense of a good life is the grace of God . . . that to which it is given is solely and simply grace.[10]

This explains why Jesus says to his disciples that it is impossible for anyone to enter the kingdom, though with God all things are possible (Matt. 19:24, 26)—with God's enabling grace this is possible. Surpassing righteousness is possible but only through God's enabling; the *doing* must be God's doing!

A NEW WAY OF LIVING

Pre-conversion works are not able to save anyone. Anybody wanting to become a Christian can never do *any* work that will make them right with God. Since they still remain outside of God's enabling grace, any work they might drum up, regardless of how good, is earthly, unspiritual, contrary to faith in God, and opposed to God's grace.

Nevertheless God has prepared works in advance for Christians to do. They are only possible because Christians are now in Christ and have the Holy Spirit inside of them, God himself—the same power that raised Jesus from the dead. Since they have become Christians by God's grace, this grace is now at work in their lives teaching them to say "no" to ungodliness and all sorts of unfruitful passions.

For this reason, it is quite impossible that a Christian would be without fruit. The absence of fruit indicates the absence of grace. A new or changed life is inevitable since, according to John Calvin, "where Christ is, there too is the Spirit of holiness, who regenerates

---

10. Augustine *Grace and Free Will* 8.19–20 (in *A Select Library of the Nicene and Post-Nicene Fathers of the Christian Church,* ed. Philip Schaff, vol. 5 (Grand Rapids: Eerdmans, 1979).

the soul to newness of life."[11] All the same, we must remember that while eternal life may be said to be "the recompense of works, it is bestowed by the gratuitous gifts of God."[12] Along the same lines Augustine declared that at the judgment God would "crown not so much thy merits, as *His own gifts*."[13] Good works are a gift from God, not an earned merit whereby we gain entry to heaven. Where then is the boasting? It is in God!

My Works, But Not My Works

When I was a young boy growing up on a farm in New Zealand I was eager to drive the tractor, mow the lawn, and exercise other duties "befitting a man." These were things that were really beyond my ability. My father would still let me do them, but not without his enabling. When I drove the tractor I would sit up on the seat with him behind. He would be there gently guiding the steering wheel. When I mowed the lawn I would stand up in between his arms and the lawn-mower and push the mower, with him providing the power right behind me. Who was I fooling to think that I could drive a tractor or push a lawn-mower by myself at such a young age? I knew very well that I could not be doing these things without the enabling hands of my father.

This is what it is like with Christian works. We are expected to do things beyond our ability, yet do them we must. We depend on our heavenly Father's enabling hands, for apart from him we can't, indeed we won't, obey. Praise God, for "his divine power has given us

---

11. John Calvin, *Selected Works of John Calvin: Tracts and Letters*, ed. Henry Beveridge and Jules Bonnet, vol. 1 (Grand Rapids: Baker, 1983), 45.
12. Calvin, *Institutes*. 3.18.4.
13. Augustine "On the Same Words of the Apostle, Phil 3 . . .," in *Sermons on Selected Lessons of the New Testament*, A Library of Fathers of the Holy Catholic Church, Anterior to the Division of the East and the West, vol. 2 (Oxford: John Henry Parker, 1844).

everything we need for life and godliness through our knowledge of him who called us by his own glory and goodness" (2 Pet. 1:3).

CHAPTER THREE

FAITH AND SALVATION: DO THEY ALWAYS GO TOGETHER?

In order to understand why, according to Jesus, no one will enter heaven without producing fruit, we need to grasp four things. To recap the first two: First, the fruit necessary for salvation *only* occurs within a relationship with God. Unbelievers cannot produce such fruit. Second, fruit is not the result of human effort per se but of God's enabling grace. It is a gift from God. It has nothing to do with earning salvation since, at the judgment, God will, in Augustine's words, "crown not so much thy merits, as His own gifts." In this chapter, I will address the third and fourth clues as to why God requires fruit to enter eternity.

FAITH—TWO PERSPECTIVES

Before I became a Christian I attended a youth rally where the speaker invited to the front those who wanted to become Christians. He said, "All you must do is *believe*." I remember so clearly thinking, "I must be saved *because I do believe*." I had grown up going to church and Sunday school and so believed in Jesus. I was not saved, though—and deep down I knew it.

A few weeks later and still not a Christian, I was on holiday with some Christian friends. It was New Year's Eve and I was sitting by myself in—unbeknown to me—a Christian café. A guy sat beside me and asked if I was a Christian. So I lied! But immediately after that I met up with a friend and asked him what I needed to do to become a Christian. My friend replied, "You must be *committed*!" That was the end of that. I wasn't committed, and I didn't want to be.

It seemed that I had been given two different answers on how to be saved. One said all I needed to do was *believe*, the other said I had to be *committed*. Which was it?

The Importance of Faith

It's quite clear: "Everyone who *believes in him* may have eternal life. For God so loved the world that he gave his one and only Son, that whoever *believes in him* shall not perish but have eternal life. . . . Whoever *believes in him* is not condemned, but whoever *does not believe* stands condemned already because he *has not believed* in the name of God's one and only Son. . . . Whoever *believes in the Son* has eternal life, but whoever rejects the Son will not see life" (John 3:15–16, 18, 36). Thus "everyone who looks to the Son and *believes in him* shall have eternal life . . . he who *believes* has everlasting life" (John 6:40, 47). "He who *believes in me* will live, even though he dies" (John 11:25).

Thus, Jesus tells a woman, "Your *faith* has saved you; go in peace" (Luke 7:50). He says we will die in our sins if we do not *believe* (John 8:24). Therefore, "to all who received him, to those who *believed in his name,* he gave the right to become children of God" (John 1:12).

On the surface this all seems clear enough—if it were not

for the fact that "many people saw the miraculous signs [Jesus] was doing and *believed in his name*" (John 2:23). We can hardly miss the word-for-word parallel with John 1:12 just quoted. These people believed in Jesus' name, thus we expect that Jesus will give them "the right to become children of God." But that's not what he does. Rather "Jesus would not entrust himself to them" (John 2:24). Quite clearly, faith does lead to salvation, *but not all faith leads to salvation.* Why?

Two Types of Faith

It may surprise you to learn that the Bible speaks of two kinds of faith.

Genuine Faith

Genuine faith leads to salvation. Here are some examples:

> These are written that you may *believe* that Jesus is the Christ, the Son of God, and that by *believing* you may have life in his name (John 20:31).

> *Believe* in the Lord Jesus, and you will be saved (Acts 16:31).

> This righteousness from God comes through *faith* in Jesus Christ to all who *believe* (Rom. 3:22).

> I have been reminded of your *sincere* faith, which first lived in your grandmother Lois and in your mother Eunice and, I am persuaded, now lives in you also (2 Tim. 1:5).

> My brothers, as *believers* in our glorious Lord Jesus Christ (James 2:1).

False Faith

We have already seen examples where faith does not save

(Matt. 7:21–23; John 2:23–24; 8:31, 44; Acts 8:13, 23). Here are some others:

> By this gospel you are saved, if you hold firmly to the word I preached to you. Otherwise, you have *believed* in vain (1 Cor. 15:2).

> What good is it, my brothers, if a man claims to have *faith* but has no deeds? Can such *faith* save him (James 2:14)?

> *Faith* by itself, if it is not accompanied by action, is dead (James 2:17).

> You *believe* that there is one God. Good! Even the demons *believe* that—and shudder (James 2:19).

What's the Difference?

So what's the difference between genuine saving faith and false faith that will save no one? There are at least seven clear differences.

Genuine Faith Involves Confession

Genuine faith involves confessing (or acknowledging) Jesus.

> If you *confess* with your mouth, "Jesus is Lord," and *believe* in your heart that God raised him from the dead, you will be saved. For it is with your heart that you *believe* and are justified, and it is with your mouth that you *confess* and are saved (Rom. 10:9–10).

Paul is not saying that confession and belief are identical. Yet neither is he saying they are separate, as if you could believe and not confess, or confess and not believe; as if you could be justified and not saved, or saved and not justified—preposterous! What he means is that you can't have faith without confession.

Jesus' own claims must be believed and confessed: "If you do not believe that I am the one I claim to be, you will indeed die in your sins" (John 8:24). Faith must then confess that Jesus is: from heaven (John 8:23), the bread that has come down from heaven to provide eternal life to those who feed on him (John 6:51), the "light of the world" to expose sin and reveal truth (John 8:12; 9:5), the "gate" to God (John 10:7, 9), the "good shepherd" who dies for his sheep (John 10:11–14), God's Son (John 10:36), "the resurrection and the life" (John 11:25), "the way and the truth and the life" (John 14:6), the "vine" and source of all fruitfulness (John 15:1, 5), and finally "I am" (John 8:58).

Genuine Faith is Objective

Saving faith must be in Jesus. It is only those who believe *in him* that have eternal life (John 3:15–16). "Whoever believes *in the Son* has eternal life" (John 3:36). "I am the resurrection and the life. He who believes *in me* will live" (John 11:25).

I am not being pedantic here. Faith that is not in Jesus will not save; when the disciples ask Jesus to "increase our faith" Jesus responds by saying all they need is "faith as small as a mustard seed" (Luke 17:5–6). The amount of faith is not important. I may have great faith in thin ice, yet all the faith in the world will not prevent that ice from cracking under my weight. On the other hand, I may have very little faith in thick ice, yet the thick ice will always hold me. The object of our faith is what counts. Faith must always be in Jesus!

Genuine Faith is Confidence

Confessing Jesus begins with believing that he is. Genuine faith, of course, must move beyond simply believing in the fact of Jesus since even the demons believe "there is one God . . . and shudder" (James 2:19). The difference between demons and Christians is that Christians believe *in* Jesus (e.g., Acts 16:31; 1 John 3:23).

If someone says to you, "I believe *in* you," they are saying "I have *confidence* in you." Thus, faith is confidence. This is why faith and doubt are so often pitted against each other (Matt. 21:12). In the midst of a storm at sea, Jesus asked his disciples, "Why are you so afraid? Do you still have no faith?" (Mark 4:40). Fear and doubt are contrary to faith. Hence, Jesus told a synagogue ruler, "Don't be afraid; just believe" (Mark 5:36).

If I believe in you I cannot at the same time fear or doubt you. This is why the writer of Hebrews does not describe faith as, "being *fearful* of what we hope for and *uncertain* of what we do not see." Rather he writes, "being *sure* [confident] of what we hope for and *certain* of what we do not see" (Heb. 11:1). The essence of faith is surety and certainty.

Genuine Faith Continues

Saving faith must last the distance. This is most clearly seen in John 6 where Jesus describes himself as the "bread of life." Anyone who wants life must *eat* of this bread. They must also *drink* his blood. Those who eat and drink *remain* in Jesus. They must *feed* on him and they "will live." Jesus concludes, "I tell you the truth, he who *believes* has everlasting life" (John 6:51, 53, 54, 56, 57). The point is quite clear: to eat, drink, remain, feed, and believe amount to the same thing, and they all result in eternal life. You will notice of these five terms from John 6 "remain" occurs smack in the middle.

Remain is the key to understanding eating, drinking, feeding, and believing. To remain is to continue. Eating, drinking, and feeding are continuous actions. Those who want eternal life must continue to feed on Jesus; they must also continue to believe. Paul says the same:

> But now he has reconciled you by Christ's physical body through death to present you holy in his sight, without blemish and free from accusation—*if you continue in your*

faith, established and firm, not moved from the hope held out in the gospel (Col. 1:22–23).

It is not good enough to "believe for a while, but in the time of testing . . . fall away" (Luke 8:13). This does not mean that faith must be impeccable. Remember the father who said to Jesus, "I do believe; help me overcome my unbelief!" (Mark 9:24). Even Abraham, who Paul said "did not waver through unbelief" (Rom. 4:20), did waver more than once (see Gen. 17:17). The point is that faith must be present over the long haul. It must continue.

Genuine Faith is Seen

When four men lower their paralyzed friend through a roof, each of the Synoptic writers say that "Jesus *saw* their faith" (Matt. 9:2; Mark 2:5; Luke 5:20). This is remarkable as we do not usually think of faith as something to be seen. Jesus, by contrast, cannot think of faith that can't be seen. He is therefore *looking* for faith. He wants to find it. "When the Son of Man comes, will he find faith on the earth?" (Luke 18:8). He found it in a Roman centurion, saying "I have not *found* anyone in Israel with such great faith" (Matt. 8:10).

Faith must be seen. James says, "I will show you my faith by what I do" (James 2:18). Isn't this obvious? Obedience requires faith. If I do not obey, it is because I lack faith; I believe my way is better than God's way. "You rebelled against the command of the Lord your God. You did not trust him or obey him" (Deut. 9:23).

Genuine Faith Leads to Relationship

John wrote his gospel so that people might "believe that Jesus is the Christ, the Son of God, and that by believing you may have life in his name" (John 20:31). Belief leads to life. But what is life? The answer is in John 17:3: "This is eternal life: that they may *know you*, the only true God, and Jesus Christ." So if believing leads to life, and life is knowing Jesus, then believing leads to knowing Jesus.

John 20:31	Believe	➔	Life
John 17:3	Life	➔	Knowing God/Jesus

But "know" means more than having mere head knowledge. Jesus asked Philip, "Don't you *know* me, Philip, even after I have been among you such a long time?" (John 14:9). Since Philip had been with Jesus "such a long time," Jesus is suggesting something more than head knowledge. Knowing Jesus means a personal relationship (cf. Gen. 4:1). Now we can understand why it is that Jesus will say to some at the judgment, "I never *knew* you" (Matt. 7:23). Genuine faith leads to relationship.

Genuine Faith Sees Jesus as Glorious

Recently, friends (and neighbors) of mine asked me why I was a Christian. After all the reasoning and logic and so forth, all I could say was "God is beautiful!" In other words, he's glorious and he's glorious in his Son. Unbelievers just don't see that. To them God is boring. They get more pleasure from a movie or a vacation or a boating trip than they do from God. They certainly cannot relate to what David meant when he said, "You have made known to me the path of life; you will fill me with joy in your presence, with eternal pleasures at your right hand" (Ps. 16:11).

This faith involves loving God with our whole being. When the lawyer asks Jesus "what must I do to inherit eternal life?" the answer is, "Love the Lord your God with all your heart and with all your soul and with all your strength and with all your mind." (Luke 10:25–27). Peter sees believing and loving Jesus as intertwined: "Though you have not seen him, you *love* him; and even though you do not see him now, you *believe* in him and are filled with an inexpressible and glorious joy" (1 Pet. 1:8). To put it plainly, you can't believe in Jesus without loving him.

More needs to be said here. There is a danger in understanding faith as a trait that belongs merely to the mind. I hope that what

I've said about genuine faith being confidence in Christ makes it clear that this isn't so. If nothing else, the idea that Jesus must be embraced as glorious certainly should awaken us to this reality. Jesus must be embraced as beautiful, and this cannot be reduced to the mind. That's surely part of the reason why Paul said that we must not only believe with the mouth but with the *heart* (see above). The emotions must be engaged if saving faith is to be present.

This is confirmed in John 6:35 where Jesus declares, "I am the bread of life. He who comes to me will never go hungry, and he who believes in me will never be thirsty." Notice the structure of this verse:

> He who *comes* to me will never go hungry,
> He who *believes* in me will never be thirsty.

The first thing to notice is that coming and believing are synonymous concepts. To believe in Christ you must come to him. Why must you come to him? Because if you do you "will never go hungry" and "will never be thirsty." To not be hungry or thirsty is to be satisfied. When one believes in Christ they must do so with the feeling and mindset that Christ will satisfy their every desire and need.[1] "Being persuaded that Christ and his promises are factual is not by *itself* saving faith"[2] for even the demons believe that much (James 2:19). Embracing Christ as glorious, "we must have a spiritual 'taste' that he is gloriously precious beyond all competing values and treasures."[3] Those who believe must simply embrace Christ with their whole beings, not just their mind.

The reason why some believed and yet were not saved at the end of John 2 is because their eyes were on the miracles, a fact obviously

---

1. I am indebted to John Piper, *What Jesus Demands of the World* for my thoughts on John 6:35.
2. John Piper, *The Purifying Power of Living by Faith in Future Grace* (Sisters, Oregon: Multnomah, 1995), 200.
3. Ibid., 202.

reflected in their hearts (John 2:24b–25). But earlier in John 2, Jesus performed another miracle, and there John tells us that Jesus "revealed his glory, and his disciples put their faith in him" (John 2:11). Thus the disciples see a miraculous sign and believe while others see miraculous signs, also believe, yet are not saved. Why? The difference is that the disciples saw Jesus' *glory* while the others did not. The connection between faith and glory is evident elsewhere in John.

Later Lazarus gets sick and dies. When Jesus finally arrives and gives orders to have the stone removed from where Lazarus is buried, he exclaims, "Did I not tell you that if you *believed,* you would see the *glory* of God?" (John 11:40). On another occasion after Jesus had done many miracles, many would not believe (John 11:37). John cites Isaiah to show why they would not believe. They cannot see or understand (John 12:38–40). They cannot see "Jesus' *glory*" (John 12:41).

The difference is glory (see 2 Cor. 4:4, 6)! Salvation takes place when the eyes of our heart and mind are opened to see Jesus for who he is and not for the miracles he can do. Hence, John Piper writes, "The glory of God in Christ, revealed though the gospel, is a real, objective *light* that must be spiritually seen in order for there to be salvation. If it is not seen—spiritually tasted as glorious—Satan still has his way, and there is no salvation."[4] To those who believe, Jesus is "precious" (1 Pet. 2:7).

Expressions of the Heart

My aim here has been to show that Christian saving faith cannot be reduced to mere intellectual belief in God's existence or even in

---

4. John Piper, *God is the Gospel: Meditations on God's Love as The Gift of Himself* (Wheaton: Crossway, 2005), 64.

Jesus' death, burial, and resurrection. Not that genuine faith does not include these things of course (cf. e.g., Heb. 11:6).

We need to be clear though. The characteristics of genuine faith are not additions to faith. It's not faith plus confession, confidence, relationship, and so on. Faith is *expressed* in these things. Faith without expression is like praise without verbal acknowledgement. (If I enjoy my wife's cooking, I've just got to tell her.) It's like happiness without a smile or sadness without tears; like love without action. Love moves people beyond words or tongue to actions and truth (e.g., 1 John 3:17–18; 2 Cor. 5:14). The same is true of genuine faith.

Salvation: What Does it Mean?

The fourth and final clue as to why fruit is necessary for salvation is Jesus' understanding of salvation. There is perhaps no greater term in the entire Bible than "salvation." Yet have you ever given much thought to its meaning? Would you ever imagine that perhaps you haven't fully understood it? Let's test this. What do you think when you read the following Bible passages?

> He who stands firm to the end will be *saved* (Matt. 10:22).

"What! I thought we were saved in the beginning. I have *already* been saved. *I* was saved in January 1987."

> "Lord, are only a few people going to be *saved*?" He said to them, "Make every effort to enter through the narrow door, because many, I tell you, will try to enter and will not be able to" (Luke 13:23–24).

"But why do we have to make *any* effort to be saved?"

> For whoever wants to *save* his life will lose it, but whoever loses his life for me and for the gospel will *save* it (Mark 8:35).

> "I never knew I had to lose my life to be saved."

>> Zacchaeus stood up and said to the Lord, "Look, Lord! Here and now I give half of my possessions to the poor, and if I have cheated anybody out of anything, I will pay back four times the amount." Jesus said to him, "Today *salvation* has come to this house, because this man, too, is a son of Abraham" (Luke 19:8–9).

> "But isn't this salvation by works?"

>> Jesus said to the woman, "Your faith has *saved* you; go in peace" (Luke 7:50).

> "Finally, a verse that makes sense!"

Salvation: What Does Jesus Say?

There is much we could say concerning salvation[5] but I wish to confine myself to making two points. The first is that salvation must be thought of holistically—that is, past, present, and future. Salvation has begun, but it has not yet finished. The second point is that salvation is always two-sided. That is, we are always saved *from* something (sin, Satan, hell, etc.) *to* something (holiness, God, heaven, etc.). First we need to see that salvation and the kingdom are essentially the same.

Salvation = the Kingdom

> Then Jesus said to his disciples, "I tell you the truth, it is hard for a rich man to enter the *kingdom* of heaven. Again I tell you, it is easier for a camel to go through the eye of a needle than

---

5. For a thorough treatment of salvation in the New Testament see E. M. B. Green, *The Meaning of Salvation* (Philadelphia: Westminster, 1965).

for a rich man to enter the *kingdom* of God [in other words, impossible!]" (Matt. 19:23–24).

When the disciples heard this, they were greatly astonished and asked, "Who then can be *saved*?" Jesus looked at them and said, "With man this [that is, to be saved] is *impossible* but with God all things are possible" (Matt. 19:25–26).

Clearly, Jesus and his disciples are interchanging kingdom and salvation.

Jesus' invitation to "*Enter* through the narrow gate . . . that leads to *life*" (Matt. 7:13–14) also means that he views (eternal) life and the kingdom as being one and the same, as the following table shows.[6]

TABLE 1: ENTERING LIFE = ENTERING THE KINGDOM

Matthew 5:20	Matthew 7:13-14	Matthew 7:21
Unless your righteousness surpasses . . . you will certainly not *enter* the *kingdom* of heaven.	*Enter* through the narrow gate . . . small is the gate and narrow the road that leads to *life*.	Not everyone who says to me, "Lord, Lord," will *enter* the *kingdom* of heaven.

Many other passages suggest the same equation between eternal life and the kingdom. For example, at the end of the age Jesus will

---

6. This is contrary to Robert Govett, *Entrance into the Kingdom: Or Reward According to Works* (Fletcher & Son, 1870; reprint, Miami Springs, FL: Schoettle, 1978), who claims that entrance into the kingdom of heaven and the reception of eternal life are distinct (see esp. pp. 134–35). There is no such distinction in Matt. 5:29 ("It is better for you to lose one part of your body than for your whole body to be thrown into hell"), which surely refers to a person who lacks surpassing righteousness and does not enter the kingdom (Matt. 5:20).

say to the "righteous," "Take your inheritance, the *kingdom* prepared for you" and the righteous will go "to *eternal life*" (Matt. 25:34, 37, 46). These same parallels hold true for "kingdom" and "salvation." To enter the kingdom one must believe (Matt. 18:3; Luke 18:16–17). One either enters "the kingdom of God" or is "thrown into hell" (Mark 9:47). Those outside the kingdom are lost (Matt 10:6–7) while those in the kingdom are reconciled to God (cf. Matt. 8:11–12; Mark 14:25; Luke 13:29).

Salvation is Past, Present, and Future

Salvation is past. Jesus assures a sinful woman that her "sins are forgiven" (Luke 7:48), then "your faith has *saved* you" (Luke 7:50). Thus, she was saved when her sins were forgiven.

Salvation is present. Jesus said to Zaccheus, "*Today,* salvation has come to this house" (Luke 18:9). So whoever believes "has eternal life" now (John 5:24a; cf. also 3:36; 6:47; 17:3). They have "crossed over from death to life" (John 5:24b; cf. 1 John 3:14). In English, "crossed" sounds like it happened in the past. This is true. But the tense of the Greek verb (the perfect tense) indicates the crossing continues. We might imagine someone who has walked into a river but is still crossing the same river. Eternal life then constitutes a relationship with the Father and the Son *now:* "This is eternal life: that they may know you, the only true God, and Jesus Christ, whom you have sent" (John 17:3; cf. 5:12).

Salvation is future. "He who stands firm to the end, *will* be saved" (Matt. 10:22; cf. 24:13; Mark 13:13). At "the renewal of all things, when the Son of Man sits on his glorious throne" (Matt. 19:28) he will say to those "blessed by my Father; take your inheritance, the kingdom prepared for you since the creation of the world" (Matt. 25:34). Then they "will eat at the feast in the kingdom of God" (Luke 14:15). People will want to enter the kingdom "on that day" (Matt. 7:22). It is this day that someone has in mind when they ask

Jesus, "Lord, are only a few people going to be saved?" (Luke 13:23), that is, "take their places at the feast in the kingdom of God" (Luke 13:29).

Salvation is Always to a New Life

We are accustomed to thinking of salvation as being saved from death, hell, sin, and so forth. Though this is certainly true, salvation always has two sides to it. We are never just saved *from* something but *to* something. Salvation, when viewed holistically, cannot be confined to a past moment in time. There is still the *toward-ness* of salvation to come.

FIGURE 4: SALVATION *FROM* AND *TO*

SALVATION

FROM → *TO*

This pattern is found in Exodus where God saves his people *from* servitude under Pharaoh *to* servitude under God (Exod. 19:1–15). Over and over Pharaoh is urged by Moses to let God's people go, so that they may "worship" God (Exod. 5:1; 7:16; 8:1, 20; 9:1, 13; 10:3; cf. 10:7–8, 11, 24, 26; 12:31). God's purpose in saving Israel was not merely deliverance *from* Egypt, but deliverance *to* God.

The exodus from Egypt provides the framework for Luke as he thinks through the salvation that God has brought to his people in Jesus. God "has raised up a horn of salvation" to save his people "*from* our enemies and *from* the hand of all who hate us . . . to rescue us *from* the hand of our enemies" (Luke 1:69, 71). He does not stop there, for Jesus also came *"to* enable us to serve him without fear in holiness and righteousness before him all our days" (Luke 1:75).

Salvation in the New Testament

As we put these two truths together—salvation being past, present, and future, as well as a *from* and *to* experience—it is best to think of salvation as a pilgrimage or a journey rather than a moment-in-time occurrence. In today's popular religious culture, salvation is normally thought of as something we acquire up front. With salvation behind us, we move on to discipleship. In Scripture a different picture emerges: One must not only enter through the small gate but also *travel* the narrow "road that leads to life" (Matt. 7:14). The entire New Testament supports this idea. Let me sketch a few examples.

Paul[7] can speak of salvation as past: God "*saved* us, not because of righteous things we had done. . . . He *saved* us through the washing of rebirth and renewal by the Holy Spirit" (Titus 3:5). Yet he also urges Christians to "continually work out your salvation" (Phil. 2:12). Why? Because their salvation is not yet finished. Christians are still "*being* saved" (1 Cor. 1: 18). This is not to say that we have not been saved, for "it is by grace you *have been saved*" (Eph. 2:8). But even here the Greek tense (perfect tense) indicates that salvation continues in the present.

What might be most surprising is that Paul typically speaks of salvation as still future—the "kingdom of God" (1 Cor. 6:9; Gal. 5:21), eternal life (Rom. 2:7; Gal. 6:8), the "day of the Lord" (1 Cor. 5:5). Only then "shall we be saved from God's wrath" (Rom. 5:10) and "destruction" (Phil. 1:28; 2 Thess. 2:10), and "share in the

---

7. See E. M. B. Green, *The Meaning of Salvation* (Philadelphia: Westminster, 1965), 152–89.

glory of our Lord Jesus Christ" (2 Thess. 2:12–13) and "his heavenly kingdom" (2 Tim. 4:18). Hence "our salvation is nearer now than when we first believed. The night is nearly over; the day is almost here" (Rom. 13:11–12).

For this reason, Paul describes the Christian life as a "walk." "For we ourselves are God's workmanship, created in Christ Jesus for good works . . . in order that we might *walk* in them" (Eph. 2:10, my translation; cf. Gal. 5:16; Col. 2:6).

In the book of Hebrews, salvation is mainly future. "Angels" are "sent to serve those who *will* inherit salvation" (Heb. 1:14), which consists of "the powers of the coming age" (Heb. 6:5), "the good things that are coming" (Heb. 10:1), "the world to come" (Heb. 2:5) and "the city that is to come" (Heb. 13:14). Christ will bring this salvation when he comes again (Heb. 9:28).

Christians are urged, therefore, to treat this life as "the race marked out for us" (Heb. 12:1). We have begun the race (Heb. 6:1a), but we are to "go on" and complete it (Heb. 6:1b). For it is only those who "end" the race that can be sure of salvation (Heb. 6:11). Only they will share in Christ (Heb. 3:14). Yes, we have come to the heavenly Jerusalem, but we are still to seek "the city that is to come" (Heb. 13:14).

Peter addresses his readers as "strangers (or pilgrims) in the world" (1 Pet. 1:1) because this world is not their home, heaven is. This life is therefore a sojourn, and Christians are pilgrims on a journey which ends in heaven. To be sure, salvation has a beginning (1 Pet. 1:1–3, 18), but Christians must "grow up" into their salvation (1 Pet. 2:2). The goal is "the salvation of your souls" (1 Pet. 1:9), which will be "revealed in the last time" (1 Pet. 1:5) "when Jesus Christ is revealed" (1 Pet. 1:13) and it will be glorious (1 Pet. 5:1, 10).

Summary: Salvation is a Pilgrimage

In the New Testament, salvation is presented as a pilgrimage. Very rarely is the word "save" or "salvation" used to refer to a past event; more often than not, the writers have future salvation in view, that is, heaven. We should therefore think of salvation holistically—beginning to end. When we think of a tree we do not think of a seed but of the tree it will become. Thus, we are on the narrow road (Jesus), the race (Hebrews), and a sojourn (Peter). We are therefore to remain (Jesus), walk (Paul), and run (Hebrews).

FIGURE 5: SALVATION IN THE NEW TESTAMENT

| *Conversion* | A Pilgrimage ⟶ | *Heaven* |

This is tremendously important for understanding why it is that no one will be saved who has not exhibited fruit. When Martin Luther says, for example, that works are necessary for salvation, he is not thinking of conversion but final salvation into heaven. When Jesus says that one must stand firm till the end to be saved, he is meaning saved in the sense of entering eternity. Similarly, surpassing righteousness is required, not to be justified or converted, but to enter into the kingdom of heaven. Another way of saying this is that those who have become Christians—saved/converted/justified—*will* bear fruit necessary for final salvation. So let's be clear: We are "not justified by obedience," wrote Luther, "nevertheless, faith produces obedience."[8] John Calvin explains:

> The efficient cause of our salvation is placed in the love of God the Father; the material cause in the obedience of the Son; the instrumental cause in the illumination of the Spirit, that is, in faith; and the final cause in the praise of the divine goodness. In this, however, *there is nothing to prevent the Lord from embracing works as inferior causes.* But how so? In this way: Those whom in mercy he has destined for the inheritance of eternal life, he, in his ordinary administration, *introduces to the possession of it by means of good works* . . . For this reason, *he sometimes makes eternal life a consequence of works.* . . . [Good works] is a kind of step to that which follows.[9]

This is the reason Peter urges us to "be all the more eager to make [our] calling and election sure. For if you do these things, you will never fall, and you will receive a rich welcome into the eternal kingdom of our Lord and Savior Jesus Christ" (2 Pet. 1:11–12). Salvation isn't over yet! We need to run this race in such a way as to make our salvation and place in heaven sure.

What Others are Saying

I know that to some of you this may sound odd. I have no doubt that the idea of a round earth sounded very odd to those who believed it was flat. Yet today we wouldn't think anything else. There are many who have studied salvation in the Bible who wouldn't think of it in any other way than a pilgrimage. According to seminary professors

---

8. Martin Luther, *Luther's Works*, vol. 44, ed. Helmut T. Lehmann (Philadelphia: Muhlenberg Press, 1955), 298.
9. John Calvin, *Institutes of the Christian Religion,* trans. Henry Beveridge, vol. 2 (Grand Rapids: Eerdmans, 1975), 3.14.21.

Thomas Schreiner and Ardel Caneday, salvation is both "prospective" and "retrospective." Here's what they mean:

> Both the present and future dimensions of salvation should be viewed as two aspects of an indivisible whole. Almost inevitably the impression that separable parts are intended will tend to creep into readers' minds, but we must fix in our minds from the beginning that *wholes instead of parts are in view*.[10]

> Salvation is not merely a past reality; it is also our future destiny.[11]

> Almost all Christians think of salvation exclusively in terms of the past. Believers often say, "I have been saved". . . . [M]ost evangelical Christians do not use the word *salvation* as it is usually used in the Bible, where the term denotes our future salvation.[12]

> We conclude that it is wrong to conceive of salvation exclusively in terms of the past. . . . We are already saved, yet our salvation has not yet been completed or consummated.[13]

New Testament Professor Mark Seifrid writes:

> We sometimes think in the church that when . . . we have received forgiveness of sins . . . the whole drama is over. We sometimes think that the whole history of salvation has reached its destination when people reach initiation. But in the Gospel of Matthew this is not so. . . . This forgiveness is the

---

10. Thomas R. Schreiner and Ardel B. Caneday, *The Race Set Before Us: A Biblical Theology of Perseverance and Assurance* (Downers Grove: InterVarsity, 2001), 47 (emphasis mine).
11. Ibid.
12. Ibid., 48.
13. Ibid., 52.

beginning . . . but—alarmingly—not necessarily the ending, of the drama.[14]

Gerald Borchert, professor of New Testament studies at Princeton Theological Seminary, is well qualified on this topic having written a book titled *Assurance and Warning: The Balance between Assurance and Warning in 1 Corinthians, John, and Hebrews*. He comments:

> Those who define salvation merely in terms of justification . . . need to see the multidimensional nature of salvation. Justification or beginning the pilgrimage with Christ is not the only meaning of being saved in the New Testament. Being saved also refers to the process of becoming holy or to sanctification. In addition, being saved refers to the final experience of joining Christ in heaven. It is not all over when one joins Christ in justification. There is far more to salvation than an initial yes to Christ and a public profession of faith in Christ.[15]

Finally, Joel Green suggests that "salvation is a 'way,' a journey, a life-path, and not only or merely a point in time or a destination we seek."[16]

Is this something that modern scholarship has invented perhaps? Not at all. Seventeenth century English Puritan preacher Jeremiah Burroughs, for example, wrote:

> Conversion must not be only at one instant at first. Men are deceived in this, if they think their conversion is finished merely at first; you must be in a way of conversion to God all the days of your life.[17]

Martin Luther could also speak of justification and salvation as

---

14. Mark A. Seifrid, *Christ, Our Righteousness: Paul's Theology of Justification* (Downers Grove: InterVarsity, 2000), esp. 172–86.
15. Gerald, L. Borchert, *Assurance and Warning* (Nashville: Broadman, 1987), 206–7.
16. Green, *Salvation,* 2.
17. Jeremiah Burroughs, *The Rare Jewel of Christian Contentment* (London: Peter Cole, 1648; Edinburgh: Banner of Truth, 1964; Reprint, 1979), 143.

a process. Accordingly to Luther, justification "is the beginning of salvation."[18] Hence we "are justified daily."[19] "For we perceive that a man who is justified is not yet a righteous man, but is in the very movement or journey toward righteousness."[20]

Where Have We Gone Wrong?

Many today appear oblivious to the idea that salvation is a pilgrimage, a road to be traveled. We think of salvation as a "personal decision" occurring at a particular moment in time. Salvation then is all about "getting in" and "making the decision" rather than the life that follows. (This of course has massive implications for how we think through evangelism, doing church, the role of preaching, assurance, etc.).

Please do not misunderstand me. I am not suggesting that there is no truth to the way we commonly think of salvation. If salvation is a pilgrimage there must be an entry point. The problem is not that this is not the truth but rather that it is not the *whole* truth.

SALVATION: A PICTURE OF TENSION

A friend and student of mine went swimming in a lake one day. When the 600-meter swim proved too much for him and he realized he wasn't going to make it upon reaching the midpoint, he was at a crossroads of decision. Feeling somewhat humiliated and embarrassed, he nevertheless did the sensible thing. He waved his arms and called for help. Fortunately, two men came to his aid. At the point his lifesavers got to him he said he felt saved, though

---

18. Martin Luther, *Luther's Works,* vol. 26, ed. Jaroslav Pelikan (Philadelphia: Muhlenberg Press, 1955), 132.
19. Luther, *Works,* 34:167.
20. Luther, *Works,* 34:152.

he nonetheless realized that he was not yet safe. Not until his feet touched the shore could he finally relax in his salvation. Likewise, we are not yet saved until we touch the shores of heaven.

Accepting the Tension

It may be difficult to comprehend how we can be saved and still not yet saved. One critic referred to such a notion as "double talk."[21] Just because it is paradoxical, however, does not mean it is untrue. It poses no more of a problem than other apparent "double-talk" in the Bible. God elects some to salvation (Rom. 9:10–18) yet invites all people to believe (Rom. 10:8–15). God decreed Jesus' death (Luke 22:22a; Acts 2:23a; 4:28) but holds Judas and others personally responsible (Luke 22:22; Acts 2:23; 4:27). Paul could be "sorrowful, yet always rejoicing" (2 Cor. 6:10).

Do these ideas not sound like double-talk? Yet we accept them because we realize that they simply reflect a God of mystery and robust complexity, not confusion. Paul accepted it (Rom. 11:33–36); so did Moses: "The secret things belong to the Lord our God, but the things revealed belong to us and to our children forever, that we may follow all the words of this law" (Deut. 29:29). Mystery, secrets, double-talk, tension, conflict—they do not exist in the Bible in order that we might eliminate them, but that we might embrace God's word in obedience.

---

21. Roy B. Zuck, review of *The Race Set before Us: A Biblical Theology of Perseverance and Assurance,* by Thomas R. Shreiner and Ardel B. Caneday, *Bibliotheca Sacra* 160 (2003): 241–43.

CHAPTER FOUR

APART FROM ME YOU CAN DO NOTHING

Having looked at the four reasons why no one will enter heaven without evidence of a changed life, we are now in a position to look at what Jesus teaches about the narrow road to heaven. What does traveling that road involve?

Jesus' Commands

One of the difficulties in reading the gospels is the demanding nature of Jesus' teaching, "Be perfect . . . as your heavenly Father is perfect" (Matt. 5:48). That pretty much sums it up. Have you ever found yourself reading the gospels and not really taking Jesus' words seriously? It's not because you don't believe his words shouldn't be taken seriously, but you just wonder *how* you can.

Herein lies the problem. Jesus' teaching, especially in the synoptic gospels (Matthew, Mark, and Luke), mostly tells us what he demands of his followers. What we are not often told is *how* we are to meet these demands. We are told to be perfect as God is perfect, but we are not told how. We are told to not be angry with others, for the fires of hell beckon. But we are not told how to not be angry. We are told not to lust lest we be thrown into hell. But the question is how.

Jesus said, "Everyone who hears these words of mine and does not put them into practice is like a foolish man who built his house on sand" which "fell with a great crash" (Matt. 7:26–27). We may say, "'Lord, Lord' . . . but only he who *does* the will of my Father who is in heaven" will in actuality "enter the kingdom of heaven" (Matt. 7:21). We cannot neglect to obey Jesus' commands because they are too hard, nor can we in legalistic self-deterministic resolve to obey, "For I tell you that unless your righteousness surpasses that of the Pharisees and the teachers of the law, you will certainly not enter the kingdom of heaven" (Matt. 5:20). What are we to do?

Jesus' Commands are Impossible!

On one occasion a certain rich young ruler came to Jesus and asked him: What must he "do to inherit eternal life?" (Mark 10:17). Jesus eventually tells the young man he must sell all he has and offload the proceeds to the poor. (I shall leave an exposition of this until a later chapter.) "At this the man's face fell. He went away sad, because he had great wealth" (Mark 10:22).

After the ruler left, disappointed, Jesus commented to his disciples: "How hard it is for the rich to enter the kingdom of God!" (Mark 10:23). *Well how hard is hard?* we might ask. Difficult but possible? Hard work but achievable? Just what does Jesus mean by "hard"? "It is easier for a camel to go through the eye of a needle than for a rich man to enter the kingdom of God," Jesus responds (Mark 10:25). If a camel can make its way through the eye of a needle, then a rich person can enter the kingdom. *That's impossible,* you say. That's indeed what the disciples thought too. "Who then can be saved?" they ask (Mark 10:25). What camel could ever fit through the eye of a needle? The answer is none. It's impossible, with man that is! "But not with God; all things are possible with God" (Mark 10:27).

What then is the ultimate answer to the rich young ruler's question, "What must I do to inherit eternal life?" The answer is he can't *do* anything. It's impossible. Nonetheless, this doesn't mean he can't obey Jesus' command and sell all he has; why else would Jesus give him the command? Neither does it mean he can't inherit eternal life; he can. But inheriting eternal life is not like traveling to another country. One of the things my boys have asked me is, "Where is heaven?" "Is it in the sky?" "Can I get to it by plane?" It's difficult for them to understand that, while heaven is real, no one can simply hop on a plane or a rocket and fly there. Jesus said, "My kingdom is not of this world. . . . My kingdom is from another place" (John 18:36). The distance to eternal life is not compassable by human means.

But there is good news! God is able to make the camel go through the eye of a needle; God can do what we cannot. This is the wonder of amazing grace. The pilgrimage of salvation is all God from start to finish.

Apart From Me You Can Do Nothing

If salvation is impossible apart from God, it stands to reason that everything else is impossible apart from him. Jesus says that our relationship to him is like a vine to branches. "I am the vine; you are the branches" (John 15:5). In order for branches to produce fruit—indeed in order to survive—they need nourishment in the form of minerals that the vine takes from the soil. Take a branch away from its vine and you take away its life support. It needs to be connected to the vine. Its very life and ability to bear fruit is bound up with the vine. "No branch can bear fruit by itself; it must remain in the vine" (John 15:4).

In the same way we cannot bear fruit unless we remain in Jesus. "If a man remains in me and I in him, he will bear much fruit; apart from me you can do nothing" (John 15:5). The "nothing" that Jesus refers to is of course fruit-bearing, but it is equally true that the

SALVATION IS MORE COMPLICATED THAN YOU THINK

"nothing" is all-encompassing! We cannot even live physically apart from Jesus since "in him all things hold together" (Col. 1:17), and he sustains "all things by his powerful word" (Heb. 1:3). On a spiritual level, unless we are regenerated we remain "dead in . . . transgressions and sins" (Eph. 2:1). It really doesn't matter from which vantage point we view "nothing," it will always amount to the same thing in the end—"apart from me you can do nothing" (John 15:5).

Salvation is impossible apart from God. No wonder the apostle Paul could say that there is "no one who seeks God" (Rom. 3:11)—*not one!* And yet Jesus tells kingdom participants that they are to "*seek first his kingdom and his righteousness*" (Matt. 6:33). We cannot seek, yet we must. How can Jesus urge people to seek God when Paul tells us that no one seeks God? The answer is, "Apart from me you can do nothing." In other words, no one can seek God *apart from God's enabling.* Jesus says:

> No one can come to me unless the Father who sent me draws him (John 6:44).

> This is why I told you that no one can come to me unless the Father has enabled him (John 6:65).

Jesus urges all to come to him. "*Come to me,* all you who are weary and burdened, and I will give you rest" (Matt. 11:28). "Let the little children *come to me,* and do not hinder them, for the kingdom of heaven belongs to such as these" (Matt. 19:14). Yet the truth is that no one can come unless God enables them.

Does this mean then that we should adopt a passive "let go and let God" kind of attitude? "If I can't do anything apart from God, then I won't do anything—at least until he enables me to." This misses the point. I heard of a woman who decided she would pray only when she felt like it. The more she waited until she felt like praying, the less she felt so inclined, until her prayer life dropped off altogether.

The point is not passivity but that in our doing we must *depend upon God*. Rather than an excuse to wait until "the Spirit moves me," we must jump headlong into life's "dead air" where only a gust from the Holy Spirit can keep us aloft! Paul expresses this relationship well and eliminates any false ideas that we might have about letting go and letting God:

> Therefore, my dear friends, as you have always obeyed—not only in my presence, but now much more in my absence—continue to work out your salvation with fear and trembling, for it is God who works in you to will and to act according to his good purpose (Phil. 2:12–13).

Notice what Paul is saying: First, we are to reject passivity by continuing working, in fear and trembling even. Why? Because we are commanded to work out our salvation, an impossible feat. The camel is being commanded to go through the eye of a needle. Nevertheless, *it's a command!*

Second, God is the one who enables us to continue to work. If we were left with the bare command to work out our salvation, what a dire situation we would be in. Fortunately Paul goes on to encourage and indeed motivate us that God is animating us "to will and to *work*" (my translation). The very work Paul commands us to do can only be carried out by God's enabling.

David understood this when he prayed to God for Solomon: "Give my son Solomon the wholehearted devotion *to keep* your commands, requirements and decrees *and to do* everything to build the palatial structure for which I have provided" (1 Chron. 29:19). Augustine understood why in some places "eternal life is given in return for good works" (e.g., Rom. 2:6),[1] and why in others it is by

---

1. Augustine *Grace and Free Will* 8.19–20 (in *The Fathers of the Church: A New Translation*, ed. Joseph Deferrari, vol. 59 [Washington, DC: The Catholic University of America Press, 1968]).

grace (e.g., Rom. 4:4). Augustine found the answer in John 15:5: "Apart from me you can do nothing." We are entirely dependent upon God to do in us what we cannot do yet must do.

BLESSED ARE THOSE WHO CAN'T

Jesus' beatitudes in Matthew 5:3–10 are well known.

Blessed are the poor in spirit, for theirs is the kingdom of heaven.
Blessed are those who mourn, for they will be comforted.
Blessed are the meek, for they will inherit the earth.
Blessed are those who hunger and thirst for righteousness, for they will be filled.
Blessed are the merciful, for they will be shown mercy.
Blessed are the pure in heart, for they will see God.
Blessed are the peacemakers, for they will be called sons of God.
Blessed are those who are persecuted because of righteousness, for theirs is the kingdom of heaven.

The Kingdom Belongs To . . .

These beatitudes answer the question, "to whom does the kingdom of heaven belong?" *The beatitudes describe the repentance required to belong to the kingdom of heaven.* Take note of how these beatitudes are structured:

Blessed are the poor in spirit, *for theirs is the kingdom of heaven.*
    Blessed are those who . . .   for they will . . .
    Blessed are the . . .   for they will . . .
    Blessed are those who . . .   for they will . . .
    Blessed are the . . .   for they will . . .
    Blessed are the . . .   for they will . . .
    Blessed are the . . .   for they will . . .
Blessed are those who are persecuted, *for theirs is the kingdom of heaven.*

The beatitudes are like a sandwich. The promise in the first and last beatitude, "theirs is the kingdom of heaven," is like the bread. The six intervening promises are like the filling. What this means is that the six promises between "theirs is the kingdom of heaven" describe different aspects of the kingdom of heaven. In other words those who belong to God's kingdom will "be comforted" (e.g., Luke 16:25; Rev. 21:4), "inherit the earth" (e.g., Rev. 21:1–3), "be shown mercy" (e.g., 2 Tim. 1:18; Jude 21), "see God" (e.g., 1 Cor. 13:12; 1 John 3:2), and "will be called sons of God" (e.g., Rom. 8:19).

Notice also that the first and last beatitudes are in the present tense: "theirs *is* the kingdom of heaven" (Matt. 5:3, 10), while the middle beatitudes are in the future tense: "for they *will* . . ." (Matt. 5:4–9). What this means is that the kingdom is present, but its completion and fullness is still future. Hence, these various aspects of the kingdom are true for Christians now, though only in part, since "what we will be has not yet been made known" (1 John 3:2a).

Therefore, the beatitudes as a whole describe those who are in the kingdom. This is the same as saying the beatitudes describe those who are Christians.

The Way of Repentance

Not only does each beatitude describe an aspect of the kingdom, but the first element of each beatitude describes an aspect of repentance. This can be easily seen by comparing the structure of the beatitudes with Matthew 4:17.

Repent	for the *kingdom of heaven* is near (Matt. 4:17).
Poor in spirit . . . persecuted	for theirs is the *kingdom of heaven* (Matt 5:3, 10).

The common element between the beatitude promises and Jesus' message in Matthew 4:17 is "the kingdom of heaven." What differs is that "repent" occurs in Matthew 4:17 while the beatitudes do not mention the word "repent." However repentance is clearly what Jesus has in mind since, according to Matthew 4:17, to belong to the kingdom one must repent, whereas according to Matthew 5:3–10 to belong to the kingdom one must be "poor in spirit," "mourn," be "meek," "hunger and thirst for righteousness," and so on. The first element of each beatitude is simply a comprehensive description of what repentance looks like. Second Chronicles 7:14 is one of the most well-known descriptions of repentance in the Bible. It corresponds remarkably well to the beatitudes.

> If my people, who are called by my name, will humble themselves and pray and seek my face [Matt. 5:3–6] and turn from their wicked ways [Matt. 5:7–9], then will I hear from heaven and will forgive their sin and will heal their land (2 Chron. 7:14).

Blessed are the Poor in Spirit

In the Old Testament times those who were poor were, of course, those who lacked money and material possessions. Because they were poor they were dependent and needy, helpless and weak. Their dependency made them vulnerable, so the unscrupulous found it easy to take advantage of them. Thus, if "a poor man is shunned by all his relatives—how much more do his friends avoid him! Though he pursues them with pleading, they are nowhere to be found" (Prov. 19:7).

It is precisely these characteristics—dependence, need, helplessness, weakness, and vulnerability—that God finds endearing. He is especially responsive to the poor. So even though "evildoers frustrate the plans of the poor" it is "the Lord [who] is their refuge" (Ps. 14:6).

It is not difficult, therefore, to see how the term "poor" was sometimes used to simply describe one's dependence upon God irrespective of whether material poverty was in view. David, for example, pleaded, "I am *poor* and needy; come quickly to me, O God. You are my help and my deliverer; O Lord, do not delay" (Ps. 70:5). Elsewhere he declares, "This poor man called, and the Lord heard him; he saved him out of all his troubles" (Ps. 34:6). Asaph certainly does not have financial poverty in mind when he asks God to "not remember the lawlessness of our fathers; let your compassion come quickly to us for we have become very poor" (Ps. 78:8 in the Greek Old Testament).

God is on the side of the poor since they have no one else to help them. He will not forsake them.

Thus, when we come to the New Testament, it is to the poor who find special favor with God. "Has not God chosen those who are poor in the eyes of the world to be rich in faith and to inherit the kingdom he promised those who love him?" (James 2:5). It is to the poor that Jesus came. "The Spirit of the Lord is on me, because he has anointed me to preach good news to the poor" (Luke 4:18). This is not to say that all poor people are chosen or receive the good news, just as not all rich people reject the good news (e.g., Luke 19:1–9). The point is that the qualities produced by poverty—dependency and so forth—are desirable qualities in God's sight.

This brings us to Jesus' first beatitude, "blessed are the poor in spirit" (Matt. 5:3). The poverty in this case is not financial (though one who is poor in spirit may be financially poor) but internal, hence the qualifier "in spirit." This doesn't mean, as is sometimes suggested, that we are to be long-faced and down in the dumps in order to receive a blessing. On the contrary, poverty of spirit is something to be desired. Indeed, it is absolutely necessary for "theirs is the kingdom of heaven" (Matt. 5:3). One cannot be a Christian without being poor in spirit. Since the kingdom belongs to those who repent (Matt. 4:17), being "poor in spirit" is a mark of repentance.

> For this is what the high and lofty One says—he who lives forever, whose name is holy: "I live in a high and holy place, but also with him who is contrite and lowly in spirit, to revive the spirit of the lowly and to revive the heart of the contrite" (Isa. 57:15).

The rock-bottom of financial poverty is bankruptcy. When someone is bankrupt they are declared to be unable to pay all their outstanding debts. There is nothing in the bank. To be poor in spirit is to declare spiritually bankruptcy. It is a recognition that we are morally and spiritual impoverished. To borrow words from Paul, it is to acknowledge that deep down we are "hostile to God." We recognize that we do "not submit to God's law, nor can . . . [we] do so" (Rom. 8:7). Indeed we "cannot please God" (Rom. 8:8).

This was certainly Isaiah's reaction when he "saw the Lord seated on a throne, high and exalted, and the train of his robe filled the temple"; heavenly beings cried out 'Holy, holy, holy is the Lord Almighty; the whole earth is full of his glory'" (Isa. 6:1, 3). Overwhelmed with a real sense of his own sinfulness, Isaiah believed his time was up. "Woe to me! . . . I am ruined." Doubtless he was just wondering what it would feel like to suddenly be obliterated to a cinder. "For I am a man of unclean lips, and I live among a people of unclean lips, and my eyes have seen the King, the Lord Almighty" (Isa. 6:5). Sinners who see the glorious bank account of God recognize their own is bankrupt. And so we say with Peter, "Go away from me, Lord; I am a sinful man!" (Luke 5:8).

Practically speaking this means that we recognize and acknowledge that in ourselves we are unable to carry out Jesus' commands. We have no ability whatsoever, for example, to not lust (Matt. 5:27–28), love our enemies (Matt. 5:43–47), forgive those who sin against us

(Matt. 6:14–15), give generously (Matt. 6:19–24), not be anxious (Matt. 6:25–34), not judge (Matt. 7:1) and do to others as we would have them do to us (Matt. 7:12).

Those who are poor in spirit, therefore, acknowledge with the Psalmists that they are "poor and needy" (Ps. 40:17; 70:15; 86:1; 109:22). They are "lowly and despised" (Ps. 119:141), so they pray "may the Lord think of me" (Ps. 40:17). They plead, "Come quickly to me, O God. You are my help and my deliverer; O Lord, do not delay" (Ps. 70:5).

BLESSED ARE THOSE WHO MOURN

Those who are financially bankrupt inevitably mourn their empty bank account. Likewise those who are poor in spirit inevitably mourn their spiritual poverty. "For I am poor and needy, and my heart is wounded within me" (Ps. 109:22). So we come to the second beatitude: "Blessed are those who mourn, for they will be comforted" (Matt. 5:4).

First, we must defer to Matthew 5:3 as our framework for interpreting the following beatitudes. The blessing, expressed here as "comfort," is still the kingdom of heaven. In other words, those who enter the kingdom will be comforted. Christians enter into this comfort now since they have come to know "the God of all comfort who comforts us in all our troubles" (2 Cor. 1:3–4). This comfort, however, is certainly not what it will be when we are in heaven (see Luke 16:25). Then God "will wipe every tear from their eyes. There will be no more death or *mourning* or crying or pain, for the old order of things has passed away" (Rev. 21:4).

Second, this beatitude is not a promise to those who mourn the loss of a loved one, for not all those who mourn in that sense will enter the kingdom. Rather those who enter the kingdom are those who mourn *in spirit*. They mourn over their sin. They mourn because they have sinned against a holy God. They mourn as David did, "I know my transgressions, and my sin is always before me. Against you, you only, have I sinned and done what is evil in your sight" (Ps. 51:3–4). They mourn as the young king Josiah did when he heard God's law and "tore his robes" and "wept" in God's presence (2 Kgs. 22:11, 19).

It is worth pointing out what mourning is not. Sometimes our mourning over sin can be a selfish and prideful thing. We mourn because we feel bad about ourselves or because we have been "caught." What we really want is not so much comfort from God but a better self-esteem. Ironically, this is pride more than it is humility. King Saul exhibited this kind of repentance when Samuel confronted him about disobeying God's command to "completely destroy those wicked people, the Amalekites" (1 Sam. 15:18). Saul was indeed repentant: "I have sinned. I violated the Lord's command and your instructions. I was afraid of the people, and so I gave in to them. Now I beg you, forgive my sin and come back with me, so that I may worship the Lord" (1 Sam. 15:24–25). He certainly said the right words. However, Saul reveals the true intent of his heart when Samuel refuses to go back with him. "As Samuel turned to leave, Saul caught hold of the hem of his robe, and it tore. . . . 'I have sinned. But please honor me before the elders of my people and before Israel; come back with me, so that I may worship the Lord your God'" (1 Sam. 15:27, 30). Saul was in fact more concerned about losing face with his elders than he was about losing face with God. The apostle Paul calls this kind of repentance "worldly sorrow" that "brings death" (2 Cor. 7:10).

The kind of mourning God blesses is "godly sorrow," which "brings repentance that leads to salvation and leaves no regret" (2 Cor. 7:10). This is what God requires before he will admit anyone into his kingdom. He invites all then to "return to me with all your heart, with fasting and weeping and mourning" (Joel 2:12). "Grieve, mourn and wail. Change your laughter to mourning and your joy to gloom" (James 4:9).

Blessed are the Meek

Those who acknowledge their spiritual poverty and mourn over their sin are inevitably meek: "Blessed are the meek, for they will inherit the earth" (Matt. 5:5). But what does it mean to be meek? The best description is found in Psalm 37, which Jesus cites to form this beatitude.

Psalm 37 is an exhortation to "not fret because of evil men or be envious of those who do wrong" (Ps. 37:1); "do not fret when men succeed in their ways, when they carry out their wicked schemes" (Ps. 37:7); "do not fret—it leads only to evil" (Ps. 37:8). Rather than fretting, David urges, "*Trust* in the Lord. . . . *Delight* yourself in the Lord. . . . *Commit* your way to the Lord; *trust* in him. . . . *Be still* before the Lord and *wait patiently* for him. . . . *Refrain* from anger and turn from wrath. . . . *Hope* in the Lord. . . . *Wait* for the Lord. . . . *Take refuge* in him" (Ps. 37:3, 4, 5, 7, 8, 9, 34, 40). Notice the emphasis: trust, delight, commit, be still, wait patiently, refrain, hope, take refuge—in the Lord.

The meek person, therefore, trusts in God; he refrains from taking things into his own hands; that is, he is still, waiting patiently and hoping in the Lord, his refuge. The meek understand they cannot force God's hand and therefore don't try; instead they wait patiently on him to act.

Practically, the meek are very similar to the poor in spirit. However, there seems to be a slight progression. Those who are poor in spirit recognize their inherent inability to please God. Those who are meek, therefore, do not try to please God. They understand that their own efforts will never satisfy God for even their "righteous acts are like filthy rags" (Isa. 64:6).

Meekness is exemplified in the parable that Jesus told: "Two men went up to the temple to pray, one a Pharisee and the other a tax collector." The Pharisee was so confident of his own righteousness that he had no problem approaching God in prayer and letting God know just how good he was. Meek he was not. On the other hand, the tax collector could not even draw near to God. Rather, "he stood at a distance. He would not even look up to heaven, but beat his breast and said, 'God, have mercy on me, a sinner'" (Luke 18:10–14). This man recognized his poverty, which led him to the realization that he could do nothing worthy to approach God. His only option was to beg for mercy. That is meekness.

Blessed are Those Who Hunger and Thirst for Righteousness

The first three beatitudes describe the heart of a person who realizes his inability to please God. They may be decent themselves, but they know that there is no part of their being that has not been infected with the disease of sin (cf. Rom. 3:10–18). They can only mourn for the greatest problem of all—there is nothing *they* can do to make themselves rich—so they wait upon God.

What now? What happens when the financially bankrupt discover they have no money in the bank? They want money! What happens when someone realizes they have nothing in the bank to please God? They hunger and thirst for righteousness. "Blessed are those who hunger and thirst for righteousness, for they will be filled" (Matt. 5:6). The picture here is of someone starving for food and water. I have never been in this position. I may say at times, "I'm starving," but I know nothing of what it really means to starve. To starve is, I would imagine, to not know where the next scrap of food is coming from, or if it is coming. To starve is more than wanting food and water but it is *needing* it. If you don't get it, you will die.

The imagery is taken from Psalm 107 where the Psalmist describes some who "wandered in desert wastelands, finding no way to a city where they could settle. They were hungry and thirsty, and their lives ebbed away" (Ps. 107:4–5). Either their hunger and thirst will be satisfied, or they will die. There is only one place to turn so "they cried out to the Lord in their trouble, and he delivered them from their distress. He led them by a straight way to a city where they could settle . . . he satisfies the thirsty and fills the hungry with good things" (Ps. 107:6–7, 9). The Psalmist goes on to describe others in deep distress—people who "stumbled, and there was no one to help" (Ps. 107:12), who "drew near the gates of death" (Ps. 107:18) who "were at their wits end" (Ps. 107:27). In their helplessness they cried out to the Lord. Either deliverance would come, or they would die.

It is only when we see our spiritual poverty and our inability to deliver ourselves that we hunger and thirst for righteousness. And God does deliver. "He turned rivers into a desert, flowing springs into thirsty ground, and fruitful land into a salt waste . . . the desert into pools of water and the parched ground into flowing springs; there he brought the hungry to live, and they founded a city where they could settle. They sowed fields and planted vineyards that yielded a fruitful harvest; he blessed them . . . he lifted the needy out of their affliction and increased their families like flocks" (Ps. 107:33–38, 41).

John writes of all those who will dwell in heaven, "Never again will they hunger; never again will they thirst. . . . For the Lamb at the center of the throne will be their shepherd; he will lead them to springs of living water. . . . Never again will they hunger; never again will they thirst" (Rev. 7:14–16). We don't have to wait for heaven to have our hunger and thirst for righteousness satisfied. It begins now, as Jesus said, "I am the bread of life. He who comes to me will never go hungry, and he who believes in me will never be thirsty" (John 6:35).

Come Quickly to Help Me

In Psalm 38 David is acutely aware of some sin(s) he has committed: "I confess my iniquity; I am troubled by my sin" (Ps. 38:18). His response is one of deep repentance of the beatitude kind. For the purpose of practically understanding these first four beatitudes, it will be helpful to compare David's words with Jesus'. We must realize though that life is not so black and white. Repentance is not a step by step process as if we start with being poor in spirit and then move on to mourning and so on. All these aspects are bound up together. They overlap and intermingle. This is what we see in this Psalm.

Poor in spirit. Because of his sin David feels "bowed down and brought very *low*" (Ps. 38:6). He is "feeble and utterly crushed" (Ps. 38:8). His "wounds fester and are loathsome because of" his "sinful folly" (Ps. 38:5). It is affecting him physically: "Because of your wrath there is no health in my body; my bones have no soundness because of my sin. . . . My heart pounds, my strength fails me; even the light has gone from my eyes" (Ps. 38:3, 10). He is a man in despair: "My guilt has overwhelmed me like a burden too heavy to bear" (Ps. 38:4).

Mourn. "All day long" he "go[es] about *mourning*" (Ps. 38:6). He "groan[s] in anguish of heart" (Ps. 38:6). Things are bleak as he exclaims, "I am about to fall, and my pain is ever with me" (Ps. 38:17).

Meek. The lowliness David feels is made worse by the fact that his "friends and companions avoid" him. Even his "neighbors stay far away." His enemies seek his life (Ps. 38:11–12). God is his only hope. He "can offer no reply" to anyone. "I *wait* for you, O Lord" (Ps. 38:14–15).

Hunger and Thirst For Righteousness. Such despair leaves David longing for relief, but there's only one place it can come from. "O

Lord, do not forsake me; be not far from me, O my God. *Come quickly* to help me, O Lord my Savior" (Ps. 38:21–22).

God Saves the Helpless

This is important. One thing we may *not* say regarding those who are in God's kingdom is that they are there because they have earned it. God does *not* help those who help themselves! It is surely not insignificant that the Sermon on the Mount, recognized for its rigorous demands and high ideals, begins with a promise to those who are helpless and dependent upon God—"Blessed are the poor in spirit." Eternal life and entry into the kingdom cannot be gained apart from complete and utter dependence upon God.

Tax Collectors and Prostitutes Are Entering the Kingdom of God Ahead of You

Many religious leaders of Jesus' day did not exemplify the utter dependence required to enter God's kingdom. Their problem was that they interpreted sin in light of the law given to them through Moses (e.g., Dan. 9:11). God delighted, so it was thought, in sacrifices and burnt offerings (Mal. 2:12–13) since that is what the law stipulated. Keeping the law then became the goal (Rom. 9:31–10:3).

The problem with this is that on one level the law could be scrupulously obeyed, just as you and I might scrupulously obey all the laws of the country in which we live. Since we do not break the speed limit or steal or murder, we might then consider ourselves to be upright and obedient. Something similar went through the minds of some first century Jews. They would "make lengthy prayers" (Mark 12:40; Luke 20:47), "fast twice a week and give a tenth of all" their earnings (Luke 18:12; cf. Matt. 6:16; 23:23; Luke 11:42; Mark 12:41). They appeared "to people as righteous" (Matt. 23:28), "clean" (Matt. 23:25) and "beautiful" (Matt. 23:27). And since the law was their standard by which they measured righteousness, some became "confident of their own righteousness and looked down on everybody else" (Luke 18:9). They believed then that they were "healthy" (Matt. 9:12). They claimed, "We are not illegitimate children. . . . The only Father we have is God himself" (John 8:41). They sincerely believed they could see (John 9:41).

The reality was that these people were "blind" (Matt. 23:16, 19). Their father was not God but "the devil" (John 8:44). So they "do not enter" the kingdom of heaven (Matt. 23:13), meaning they are going to "hell" (Matt. 23:15; 33).

Their problem? A lack of recognition that sin went any deeper than disobedience to the law. They could not, it seems, say with King David, "Surely I was sinful at birth, sinful from the time my mother conceived me" (Ps. 51:5). They had somehow missed that it was not sacrifice or burnt offerings that God took pleasure in but "a broken and contrite heart" (Ps. 51:16–17), that is, a poor spirit, mourning over sin, meekness, and a hungering and thirsting after righteousness (Matt. 5:3–6).

Jesus did not come to call people who were confident of their own righteousness; he came to call "sinners" (Matt. 9:13). This is astonishing since "We know," according to some of the Jewish religious leaders, "God does not listen to sinners" (John 9:31). Remember, however, that a sinner in their mind was someone who disobeyed the law. Actually, a sinner was much more than that according to Jesus. Sin may manifest itself outwardly, but the real problem lies deep within. Thus, Jesus said, "What comes out of a man is what makes him 'unclean.' For from within, out of men's hearts, come evil thoughts, sexual immorality, theft, murder, adultery, greed, malice, deceit, lewdness, envy, slander, arrogance and folly. All these evils come from inside and make a man 'unclean'" (Mark 7:20–23).

I am often asked how is it that "innocent" babies who do not commit sinful acts can still be considered sinners? Such a question betrays a faulty understanding of sin—sin is merely what we do. Yet for as long as we think of sin this way we will not properly understand or feel our utter inability to please God. This is why it was so hard for some to comprehend that Jesus ate with "sinners."

To a fair few of the religious leaders of Jesus' day, "pagans" or "Gentiles" (cf. Luke 6:32–34 with Matt. 5:47) and "prostitutes" (Matt. 21:31–32) were all tagged with the label, "sinners." Jewish "tax collectors" were also thought of this way (Matt. 9:11; 11:19) because they broke the law by exacting more tax than they should from people (e.g., Luke 19:8), and they rubbed shoulders with Gentiles. How shocking then that Jesus would call Matthew, a Jewish tax collector, to follow him (Matt. 9:9–11) and so gained a reputation for being a "glutton and a drunkard, a friend of tax collectors and 'sinners'" (Matt. 11:19).

Jesus was not looking for righteousness, however; he was looking for a poor spirit and a hunger for true righteousness. The marginalized knew they were sinners. They could see their inner poverty, and they mourned over their sin. In meekness some could "not even look up to heaven" but with a hunger and thirst for righteousness would beat their breast and cry out, "God, have mercy on me, a sinner" (Luke 18:13). They believed and repented when confronted with "the way of righteousness," not righteousness through the law but through Jesus—a righteousness they knew they could never attain apart from him (Matt. 21:32). It is these people that Jesus calls into his kingdom; not because they are righteous, but because they know they are not and can never be apart from Jesus. These are the ones God justifies and exalts (Luke 18:14), so "tax collectors and the prostitutes are entering the kingdom of God ahead of" self-confident, law-abiding, religious people (Matt. 21:31).

Like a Little Child

Children were in a similar position to tax-collectors and prostitutes, but not because they were despicable. Rather, it was their misfortune to begin life at the very bottom of the social ladder. Increasing age brought with it increasing esteem. "Gray hair is a crown of splendor; it is attained by a righteous life" (Prov. 16:31), so people were expected to "revere those with grey hair" and give up "all privileges to aged persons" (Pseudo-Phocylides 220–21). When "little children were brought to Jesus for him to place his hands on them and pray for them . . . the disciples rebuked those who brought them" (Matt. 19:13). Being without privilege meant being without defense or power. Children were helpless. What child, for example, could defend himself against Herod when "he gave orders to kill all the boys in Bethlehem and its vicinity who were two years old and under"? (Matt. 2:16).

Given this background, Jesus employs some surprising and unexpected metaphors involving children. God hides the way of the kingdom "from the wise and learned" but reveals it "to little children" (Matt. 11:25; cf. 1 Cor. 1:26–29). This is a startling declaration in a day where grey hair engendered reverence. Just as startling would have been Jesus' response to the religious leaders who were indignant over the children running about the temple shouting "hosanna to the Son of David." "Have you never read . . . from the lips of children and infants you have ordained praise"? (Matt. 21:15–16).

Most striking of all is that Jesus requires everyone to climb back *down* the social ladder and become like a child in order to enter the kingdom (Matt. 18:1–4; 19:13–15; Mark 10:13–15; Luke 18:15–17). Imagine the surprise in a culture where old age was a sign of righteousness (Prov. 16:31). Of course, Jesus' point is not that the elderly cannot enter the kingdom, but "whoever humbles himself like this child" can enter the kingdom (Matt. 18:4). The child's inability to help himself makes him or her a prime illustration of someone who is poor in spirit. The kingdom does not belong to those who think they are "the greatest" (Matt. 18:1)—the learned, the wise, and the gray heads.

Therefore, if one is to enter God's kingdom they must "change and become like little children" (Matt. 18:3). The word "change" means "turn." What is it that we are meant to turn from? Since the disciples had just asked Jesus who would be "the greatest in the kingdom of heaven" (Matt. 18:1), the turning surely consists of turning from preconceived notions of greatness.

Christians are not great in the eyes of the world. They are poor in spirit (Matt. 5:3), meek (Matt. 5:5), merciful (Matt. 5:7), and persecuted (Matt. 5:10). They are powerless and insignificant. They are tax collectors, prostitutes, and sinners. They are humble (Matt. 23:12). They are, in the words of Henry Scougal, "in the lowest prostration of their own souls before God . . . to the bottom of their beings, and vanish and disappear in the presence of God, by a serious and affectionate acknowledgement of their own nothings, and the shortness and imperfections of their own attainments."[2]

"Brothers, think of what you were when you were called. Not many of you were wise by human standards; not many were influential; not many were of noble birth. But God chose the foolish things of the world to shame the wise; God chose the weak things of the world to shame the strong. He chose the lowly things of this world and the despised things—and the things that are not—to nullify the things that are, so that no one may boast before him" (1 Cor. 1:26–29). "Listen . . . has not God chosen those who are poor in the eyes of the world to be rich in faith and to inherit the kingdom he promised those who love him?" (James 2:5).

---

2. Henry Scougal, *The Life of God in the Soul of Man* (Fearn, UK: Christian Heritage, 1996), 87.

The Eleventh Hour

How can it be that sinners are entering into the kingdom of heaven ahead of the religious folk? The answer is found in a parable told by Jesus concerning the nature of the kingdom of heaven. "The kingdom of heaven," Jesus says, "is like a landowner who went out early in the morning to hire men to work in his vineyard. He agreed to pay them a denarius for the day and sent them into his vineyard" (Matt. 20:1–2).

Now work and employment in the first century was not like it is today where wages and salaries can by and large be depended upon at regular intervals. In first century culture, job security was a day to day affair. Men would gather early in the morning at a public spot, say the marketplace, in hopes of being selected for a day's work. Employers would show up to peruse the prospective employees and select those they wanted. Those who were fortunate enough to be chosen were guaranteed work for one day only, for which they would be normally paid one denarius. Those not selected could wait around hoping other employers would come by to repeat the process. Still there was no guarantee of work for that day. If no work was forthcoming they would simply turn up the next morning hoping to be more fortunate.

In Jesus' parable the landowner of a vineyard arrives early in the morning to hire workers for the day. He makes his selection, the standard amount of one denarius is agreed to, and they go off to work. For whatever reason, however, the landowner returns to the market place around 9:00 AM ("about the third hour") "and saw others standing in the marketplace doing nothing" (Matt. 20:3). Whether these men were waiting for a job or just loitering is hard to say. But since the day was already under way surely they must have considered their chances slim of securing work. But the landowner adds them to his crew, this time not stipulating a wage but rather, "I will pay you whatever is right" (Matt. 20:4). The assumption is that they will be paid for nine hours (9:00 AM to 6:00 PM), that is, three quarters of a denarius.

The landowner returns three hours later around lunch time ("about the sixth hour") to the market place and hires more workers (Matt. 20:5). Doubtless, these workers would have been thrilled to secure employment this late in the day. Oddly, the landowner returns again just one hour before knock off ("the eleventh hour"). He finds some men and asks them, "Why have you been standing here all day long doing nothing?" They reply, "Because no one has hired us." And so the landowner sends them off to his vineyard (Matt. 20:6–7).

"When evening came" (Matt. 20:8) the landowner, according to the law of Moses (Lev. 19:13; Deut. 24:15), told his foreman to gather together the workers and pay their wages "beginning with the last ones hired and going on to the first" (Matt. 20:8). The workers hired last obviously expected to be paid one hour's worth of a denarius, so we can imagine their surprise and delight when "each received a denarius" (Matt. 20:9), the amount promised to those who worked a full day. Not surprisingly, "when those came who were hired first, they expected to receive more. But each one of them also received a denarius" (Matt. 20:10). Therefore whether one worked a twelve hour day, a nine hour day, half a day, or just one hour, everyone got a denarius. While those hired late would have been delighted, those hired at sunrise "began to grumble against the landowner" (Matt. 20:11). Their argument: "These men who were hired last worked only one hour . . . and you have made them equal to us who have borne the burden of the work and the heat of the day" (Matt. 20:12).

Who of us would not have also grumbled? It's not that a denarius would have been too little. After all that's what they agreed on. The landowner was not being unfair (Matt. 20:13). But that's not the way these first workers looked at it. If you were in the vineyard since sunrise, wouldn't you expect a little more than the fellow who showed up an hour before quitting time? The first workers had done most of the work and, on top of that, worked through the hottest part of the day.

But the landowner simply replies, "Take your pay and go. I *want* to give the man who was hired last the same as I gave you. Don't I have the right to do what I want with my own money? Or are you envious because I am generous?" (Matt. 20:14–15). This is quite startling. Now it appears that the landowner did not in fact hire these later workers because he needed them but because *they* needed him.[3] He simply came to the market place and found these men "doing nothing" (Matt. 20:3, 6). It was only after recognizing their situation that he hired them. Hence the landowner is not merely generous because he paid these later workers as if they had worked a full day. He is generous because he did not need them to work in his vineyard in the first place.

That's what God's kingdom is like (Matt. 20:1). He calls us who are poor in spirit, who mourn over our sin, who are meek and recognize we can't come to God and yet hunger to come to him; he calls us who are sinners, tax-collectors, prostitutes; us who are humble like children. You might call us the eleventh hour people of society, those "doing nothing"—the last! Not because God needs us, but because we need him.

It's All of God

I have only wanted to communicate *one* point in this chapter—we can't, we don't have the ability, to enter God's kingdom. In fact, not only do we lack the ability, we lack the desire and understanding (Rom. 3:11). Left up to us it's all impossible! Whether it's justification,

---

3. This is the view of John Nolland, *The Gospel of Matthew*, The New International Greek Testament Commentary, ed. I. Howard Marshall and Donald A. Hagner (Grand Rapids: Eerdmans, 2005), 811.

conversion, discipleship, sanctification, good works, heaven, glorification, salvation—it doesn't matter, it's all impossible, for apart from Jesus we can do nothing. We're no better than workers standing around the market place at the eleventh hour doing nothing. We are at the grace and mercy of a generous landowner to come and call us to his vineyard.

I want you to remember this point. It needs to undergird our reading of the gospels, not to mention our entire lives. Jesus begins the Sermon on the Mount with the words, "blessed are the poor in spirit." Soon, for we will look at the rest of the Sermon on the Mount in the next chapter, we will find ourselves in the midst of some very heavy warnings—"If your right eye causes you to sin, gouge it out and throw it away. It is better for you to lose one part of your body than for your whole body to be thrown into hell" (Matt. 5:29). "Be careful not to do your 'acts of righteousness' before men, to be seen by them. If you do, you will have no reward from your Father in heaven" (Matt. 6:1). "Do not judge, or you will be judged" (Matt. 7:1).

If we fail to keep in mind the things spoken of in this chapter we will wonder what Jesus is saying. Unless we are careful to remember Matthew 5:3 ("Blessed are the poor in spirit") we may either succumb to an arduous type of legalism that takes Jesus' commands seriously but fails to understand we are unable to obey them, or we may give in to a licentious type of Christianity that recognizes correctly that Jesus' commands are impossible, so we fail to take them seriously. For even though we can't obey, we *must*. For it is only those who hear Jesus' words and put them into practice who will avoid falling "with a great crash" (Matt. 7:24, 27). But remember—"Apart from me you can do nothing!"

Do You Really Believe This?

Jeffrey Lionel Dahmer killed his first person in 1978 when he was just eighteen. The victim was a young hitchhiker whom he beat to death with a barbell and hammer. He committed his next murder in 1987—a young man he had picked up at a gay bar. The next year he was arrested on charges of sexually molesting a thirteen year old boy. He was imprisoned for ten months. Yet his insatiable desire to kill did not stop, and by July 1991 he was killing one male a week, a total of seventeen boys and men between 1978 and 1991.

I can't bring myself to write how he killed his victims. This information is readily available in books, movies, and of course there are plenty of details on the internet.[4] Truly, I have not read a more gruesome account. The first police officer in Dahmer's house was there because of an unrelated incident. He was only alerted to something being wrong when he happened to open up the door of the refrigerator and found a human head looking back at him.

Jeffrey's own father described the situation: "I could not imagine how he had become such a ruined soul. For the first time I no longer believed that my efforts and resources alone would be enough to save my son. There was something missing in Jeff. We call it a 'conscience.' That had either died or had never been alive in the first place."

After Dahmer was finally arrested, he told an investigator, "I have to question whether there is an evil force in the world and whether or not I have been influenced by it." He was charged with fifteen counts of murder to which he pleaded not guilty by reason of insanity. His plea was rejected by the court, and on February 17, 1992, he was sentenced to fifteen consecutive life sentences, a minimum of 936 years. In 1994 Dahmer was murdered by another prison inmate who claimed he was doing God's work.

---

4. See e.g., http://www.crimelibrary.com/serial_killers/notorious/dahmer/index.html (accessed 3:20 pm, January 2, 2007).

Seven months before he died, Dahmer, a homosexual, murderer, and cannibal, gave his life to Jesus Christ and was baptized by the prison chaplain, Roy Ratcliff. The chaplain visited Dahmer for seven months and became fully convinced of his conversion.

There was a public outcry. One person actually said that if Dahmer was in heaven, then he didn't want to go there. But is Dahmer's conversion, if that's what it was, any different from the tax-collectors' and prostitutes' we have read about in the gospels? The thief's on the cross? Or the apostle Paul's, who hunted down Christians and killed them, trying to destroy God's Church? Is Dahmer's conversion any different from yours or mine?

God calls sinners, and no one, whether a prostitute, a Jeffrey Dahmer, a Saul of Tarsus, or an Alan Stanley, has any right to call heaven home. Only God has that right, and he gives it to those who recognize they have nothing to offer. Do you really believe that you are spiritually impoverished to the depth of your being and that you have no more right to call God your Father and heaven home than someone like Jeffrey Dahmer? If you don't, then read Romans 3:10–12 again.

A Puritan Prayer

The Puritans were Christians who lived mainly in the sixteenth and seventeenth centuries and were known for their godly devotion and aspirations. Some of the more well known are Charles Spurgeon, John Bunyan, John Owen, and Jonathan Edwards. They not only knew their God, but they had an insightful and keen awareness into their own hearts. Below is a prayer that reveals the heart of these men in line with the things we have been discussing in this chapter.

O Lord,
Thou knowest my great unfitness for service,
    my present deadness,

    my inability to do anything for thy glory,
        my distressing coldness of heart.
I am weak, ignorant, unprofitable,
    and loathe and abhor myself.
I am at a loss to know what thou wouldest have me do,
        for I feel amazingly deserted by thee,
        and sense thy presence so little;
Thou makest me possess the sins of my youth,
        and the dreadful sin of my nature,
    so that I feel all sin,
    I cannot think or act but every motion is sin.
Return again with showers of converting grace
    to a poor gospel-abusing sinner.
Help my soul to breathe after holiness,
        after a constant devotedness to thee,
        after growth in grace more abundantly every day.
O Lord, I am lost in the pursuit of this blessedness,
And am ready to sink because I fall short of my desire;
Help me to hold out a little longer,
    until the happy hour of deliverance comes,
    for I cannot lift my soul to thee
    if thou of thy goodness bring me not nigh.
Help me to be diffident, watchful, tender,
    lest I offend my blessed friend
    in thought and behaviour;
I confide in thee and lean upon thee,
    and need thee at all times to assist and lead me.
O that all my distresses and apprehensions
    might prove but Christ's school
    to make me fit for greater service
    by teaching me the great lesson of humility.[5]

---

5. Arthur Bennett, ed., *The Valley of Vision: A Collection of Puritan Prayers and Devotions* (Edinburgh: Banner of Truth, 1975), 99.

CHAPTER FIVE

I CHOSE YOU TO BEAR FRUIT

In light of a survey carried out in 2004, George Barna, the directing leader of The Barna Group, made the following comment: "The ultimate aim of belief in Jesus is . . . to become a transformed person." Yet, Barna continues, "millions of people who rely on Jesus Christ for their eternal destiny have problems translating their religious beliefs into action beyond Sunday mornings."[1]

"The ultimate aim of belief in Jesus is to become a transformed person." This is much like what Jesus said to his disciples, "You did not choose me, but I chose you and appointed you to go and bear fruit—fruit that will last" (John 15:16). Fruit! We might think of fruit as "a transformed person" or "action beyond Sunday mornings." Or we might think of it in theological terms such as "sanctification" or "spiritual growth." Or we might think of it in biblical phrases such as "righteousness [that] surpasses that of the Pharisees" (Matt. 5:20), "transformed into his likeness with ever-increasing glory" (2 Cor. 3:18), or "conformed to the likeness of his Son" (Rom. 8:29). Or we

---

1. http://www.barna.org/FlexPage.aspx?Page=BarnaUpdate&BarnaUpdateID=164 (accessed 10:05pm, December 1, 2006).

might just think of plain words like "obedience" or "holiness." We have been chosen to bear fruit.

More on Repentance

Repentance is a Change of Mind

In the previous chapter we saw that the beatitudes describe the kind of repentance necessary for admittance into the eternal kingdom. The first four beatitudes especially emphasize the repentant condition of one's heart before God (Matt. 5:3–6). There is more to repentance, however. Often repentance gets casually described as a "change of mind." It is certainly that but it is more. It is a deep change in heart and desire.

Repentance is a Change in Direction

My boys love watching me describe repentance. I simply walk until they say "repent," at which point I turn about-face and walk in the other direction. They love it because they invariably end up shouting "Repent, repent, repent, repent," until I'm dizzy from constantly *turning* around. That's what repentance is. Once we were walking away from God. When we repent we turn about-face and walk in faith toward God. This is what the Thessalonians did: they "*turned to God from* idols to serve the living and true God" (1 Thess. 1:9). The apostle Paul "declared to both Jews and Greeks that they must *turn to God* in repentance and have faith in our Lord Jesus" (Acts 20:21). Repentance is a turning "from acts that lead to death" and a turning to "faith in God" (Heb. 6:1).

Repentance Will Always Produce Fruit

Repentance or turning is never merely internal. John the Baptist urged his hearers to "produce fruit in keeping with repentance" (Matt. 3:8; Luke 3:8). "To those in Jerusalem and in all Judea," Paul "preached that they should repent and turn to God and prove their repentance by their deeds" (Acts 26:20). Jesus warned the church in Ephesus to "repent and do the things you did at first" (Rev. 2:5). Those who "did not repent" after the seven plagues in Revelation "did not stop worshiping demons, and idols of gold, silver, bronze, stone and wood" (Rev. 9:20). Repentance brings change. A failure to repent means that life stays the same.

Repentance is a lot more than a change of mind. One who truly changes their mind about smoking, for example, will seriously attempt to stop smoking. There must be fruit in keeping with repentance. The change in direction must be concrete. The people in Jesus' day knew this, so after John the Baptist told the crowd to produce fruit in keeping with repentance, they asked him, "What should we do then?" To which John replied, "The man with two tunics should share with him who has none, and the one who has food should do the same. . . . Don't collect any more than you are required to. . . . Don't extort money and don't accuse people falsely—be content with your pay" (Luke 3:10–14).

Jesus himself taught that there must be fruit in explaining the parable of the soils (Matt. 13:3–8).

> When anyone hears the message about the kingdom and does not understand it, the evil one comes and snatches away what was sown in his heart. This is the seed sown along the path. The one who received the seed that fell on rocky places is the man who hears the word and at once receives it with joy. But since he has no root, he lasts only a short time. When trouble or persecution comes because of the word, he quickly falls away. The one who received the seed that fell among the thorns is the man who hears the word, but the worries of this life and the deceitfulness of wealth choke it, making it unfruitful (Matt. 13:19–22).

It is sometimes said that the second and third people in this parable are merely unfruitful Christians, however it is highly doubtful that they are Christians at all. First, if soils two and three were saved, we would expect, following the progression from soil one to soil two, a progression from soil two to three. Instead we see regression—the third doesn't even receive the word with joy.

Second, in passages surrounding this parable Jesus lumps humanity into two categories, not four. People are either a "good" tree or a "bad" tree (Matt. 12:33); they either do God's will or they don't (Matt. 12:46–50); they have or they don't have (Matt. 13:12); they are either "weeds" or "wheat" (Matt. 13:24–30), "wicked" or "righteous" (Matt. 13:49).

Third, it would be strange indeed for Jesus to exclude professing Christians from salvation as he so clearly does elsewhere (e.g., Matt. 7:21; 10:22; John 2:23–25) but here to include them. Jesus did not say, "by their profession you will recognize them," but "by their fruit you will recognize them"! (Matt. 7:16, 20). This parable therefore "teaches us to mistrust such professions of faith when they don't lead to substantive personal transformation."[2]

Fourth, the rest of the New Testament views these two middle soils as unbelievers. The second soil people do not persevere through trial. James writes, "Blessed is the man who perseveres under trial, because when he has stood the test, he will receive the crown of life that God has promised to those who love him" (James 1:12). (James 2:5 makes it clear that *all* believers will receive this crown since *all* believers also "inherit the kingdom promised [to] those who love him?"). Concerning the third soil John says, "If anyone loves the world, the love of the Father is not in him" (1 John 2:15). James warns, "Don't you know that friendship with the world is

---

2. Craig L. Blomberg, *Preaching the Parables: From Responsible Interpretation to Powerful Proclamation* (Grand Rapids: Baker, 2004), 113.

hatred toward God? Anyone who chooses to be a friend of the world becomes an enemy of God" (James 4:4).

It is only the fourth group in the parable who are saved: "the man who hears the word and understands it. He produces a crop, yielding a hundred, sixty or thirty times what was sown" (Matt. 13:23). Thus, "those who are true believers . . . will bear fruit of some kind."[3] Martin Luther went as far as saying, "if good works do not follow, then faith is false and not true."[4] "There may be varying amounts of yield in each person, but there must be a yield . . . so we should not just hope for transformation but should expect it."[5]

How could we not expect it? After all "no one who is born of God will continue to sin, because God's seed remains in him" (1 John 3:9).[6] One cannot have God's seed within and not grow. If there is no growth and fruit, there can only be one answer as to why not. God's seed is not present because of unbelief!

Returning to the beatitudes then, it becomes clear why Jesus does not leave the beatitudes in the heart or the mind. He goes on to the "fruit." There must be fruit if repentance is to be genuine and encompass salvation. Therefore those who repent will also, in time and to varying degrees no doubt, be "merciful . . . pure in heart . . . and peacemakers" (Matt. 5:7–9). For "the kingdom of God will be . . . given to a people who will produce its fruit" (Matt. 21:43).

---

3. Ibid., 110.
4. Robert Kolb and Timothy J. Wengert, eds., *The Book of Concord: The Confessions of the Evangelical Lutheran Church*, trans. Charles Arand et al., *Smalcald Articles* by Martin Luther (Minneapolis: Fortress, 2000), 325.
5. Michael J. Wilkins, *Matthew*, The NIV Application Commentary Series, ed. Terry Muck (Grand Rapids: Zondervan, 2004), 481, 502.
6. John does not mean that Christians will be sinless; if we think we can reach a sinless state we deceive ourselves and call God a liar (1 John 1:8, 10). Rather, Christians confess their sin (1 John 1:9). Sin is the reason we have Jesus Christ as our advocate (1 John 2:1).

Repentance Will Be Noticed

But what are we to make of the last beatitude? "Blessed are those who are persecuted because of righteousness, for theirs is the kingdom of heaven" (Matt. 5:10). What is Jesus saying? How can persecution be a pre-requisite for belonging to God's kingdom? All the other seven beatitudes can be turned into commands and obeyed, but not this one. We don't have any command that says, "Be persecuted."

In understanding the place of persecution, it is important to note the way this list of beatitudes is arranged. At a very general level these beatitudes have a progression to them. That is, they progress from an inner disposition of the heart (Matt. 5:3–6) to outward expression (Matt. 5:7–9). This does not mean that one begins with being poor in spirit and moves on to mourning over their sin and then being meek, and so forth. In reality all of these aspects of repentance are happening at once, repeatedly day after day. As words on a page, however, they have a natural progression to them.

Persecution appears last because it comes as a response from people who oppose a beatitude lifestyle, that is, a repentant lifestyle. The point is that a beatitude lifestyle will be noticed.[7] There will be two responses to the beatitude kind of life. First, people may "insult you, persecute you and falsely say all kinds of evil against you because of" Jesus (Matt. 5:11). Notice that persecution is not always full-blown and physical as we normally think when we think of persecution. There is a danger of thinking that persecution is cultural and happens outside the western world; however, insults and false accusations can happen anywhere and indeed will when a beatitude life is present.

Persecution will come to those who live contrary to society's "rules." For example, "meekness," so they say, "is a sign of weakness."

---

7. D. A. Carson, *The Sermon on the Mount: An Exposition of Matthew 5–7*, Biblical Classics Library (Carlisle, UK: Paternoster, 1994), 31.

Mercy is a rare trait in today's society. Of course, we show mercy to those we love but "even pagans do that" (Matt. 5:47). There is certainly a world-wide call to show mercy to those who are poor and vulnerable outside the West—and this is a good thing. Yet what about our own backyard? What about those strangers in our community who need help? They may not even particularly deserve help. It is uncommon to see people want to respond in mercy to people closer to home unless they are a close friend or member of the family. People who do step out and help are often mocked for being too gullible. Need I say anything about standards of purity regarding sex outside of marriage and the like?

The point is that a beatitude lifestyle cannot be hidden, just as "a city on a hill cannot be hidden." Kingdom participants are "the light of the world" (Matt. 5:14). An unnoticed beatitude life is like an unnoticed, lit up, city on a hill at night. Repentant lives get noticed, and there's the challenge: "everyone who wants to live a godly life in Christ Jesus will be persecuted" (2 Tim. 3:12)? Persecution is not cultural or optional for those living godly lives. Paul said that "We *must* go through many hardships to enter the kingdom of God" (Acts 14:22). They are as necessary as Jesus suffering and dying on the cross ("The Son of Man *must* suffer many things," Mark 8:31).

In other words opposition is the final and true test of whether we are living out these beatitudes. Without persecution some merely "receive the word with joy when they hear it, but they have no root. They believe for a while" (Luke 8:13). When trials come one's faith may either be "proved genuine" (1 Pet. 5:7) or "in the time of testing they fall away" (Luke 8:13). Persecution then is the ultimate test as to whether one's repentance is genuine.

Persecution of course may not be the only response to a repentant life. Some "may see your good deeds and praise your Father in heaven" (Matt. 5:16; cf. 1 Pet. 2:12). Thus, we need to examine ourselves if there is *no* response. This challenges me. Is my life having any impact, positively or negatively, on those around me? Is it being noticed? Is it generating a response? Or do I blend in so much that there is no response because there is no difference? "Blessed are those who are persecuted because of righteousness, for theirs is the kingdom of heaven" (Matt. 5:10).

The Fruit of Repentance: Surpassing Righteousness

The central thrust of Jesus' message on earth was, "Repent, for the kingdom of heaven is near" (Matt. 4:17). What this repentance looks like is spelled out in a general way in the beatitudes. It begins with deep conviction within the heart and mind and transforms our relationships. The change, which is not to be confused with perfection, cannot be hidden from those we rub shoulders with (Matt. 5:3–10).

Jesus picks up the theme of the kingdom again in Matthew 5:20 and in so doing provides even greater detail as to what this repentance looks like. He declares that, "unless your righteousness surpasses that of the Pharisees and the teachers of the law, you will certainly not enter the kingdom of heaven" (Matt. 5:20). What is this surpassing righteousness? It is tempting to identify this as something akin to what Paul calls "the gift of righteousness" (Rom. 5:17; cf. Rom. 4:3, 5; Phil. 3:9). We must, however, be careful that we do not confuse Paul's words with Jesus'. We must take our cue from what Jesus says, and he defines surpassing righteousness in the verses that follow (Matt. 5:21–48): reconciliation in relationships (Matt. 5:21–26), purity (Matt. 5:27–30), marital faithfulness (Matt. 5:31–32), integrity (Matt. 5:33–37), patience (Matt. 5:38–42), and love for enemies (Matt. 5:43–48).

We will look at three of these passages in the next chapter. But in each case Jesus reminds his hearers of what the Old Testament law said ("You have heard that it was said . . .") but then *surpasses* that ("But I tell you . . ."). Jesus is not changing or reinterpreting or contradicting the law. He did not come to "abolish the Law . . . but to fulfill them" (Matt. 5:17). The point is that Jesus is the ultimate interpreter of the law. The law finds its ultimate fulfillment or end in Jesus (Rom. 10:4). Jesus is everything the law was meant to be.

Quite clearly this is not the gift of righteousness that Paul speaks of. Surpassing righteousness is lived out; it is concrete, practical, and real, but we must not forget that it is a gift from God, for apart from him you can do nothing" (John 15:5).

The Father's Will

There is an obvious connection between Matthew 5:20 and 7:21 that is very helpful in getting to the core meaning of just what surpassing righteousness is.

> For I tell you that unless your righteousness surpasses that of the Pharisees and the teachers of the law, you will certainly not *enter the kingdom of heaven* (Matt. 5:20).

> Not everyone who says to me, 'Lord, Lord,' will *enter the kingdom of heaven,* but only he who does the will of my Father who is in heaven (Matt. 7:21).

Since the common element between these two verses is "enter the kingdom of heaven," it follows that "righteousness that surpasses that of the Pharisees and the teachers of the law" and "the will of my Father who is in heaven" are one and the same. To do the Father's will is to practice surpassing righteousness, in other words. To fail in this area is to miss the kingdom, "For whoever does the will of my Father in heaven is my brother and sister and mother" (Matt. 12:50).

But what is the Father's will? Certainly we should not equate this with a vocation or marriage partner. Rather, all of God's commands to us are his will. David said, "I desire to do *your will,* O my God;

your law is within my heart" (Ps. 40:8). We can, however, narrow down God's will even more.

God's will is stated two times in Matthew, and it is very clear. Jesus twice cites Hosea 6:6: "I desire (Greek = "will") mercy, not sacrifice" (Matt. 9:13; 12:7). It is surely significant as well that on both occasions Jesus is speaking to the Pharisees. God's will is foreign to them. They think that by righteousness God wants sacrifices, but Jesus requires a righteousness that surpasses mere legalistic observance of the law. God's will is bound up in mercy.

There is a connection between mercy, the Father's will, and surpassing righteousness. Mercy is at the core. This makes sense since Jesus criticizes the Pharisees for neglecting to put into practice "the more important matters of the law—justice, *mercy* and faithfulness" (Matt. 23:23) and because of that are not entering the kingdom (Matt. 23:13). Furthermore, at the final judgment what separates the sheep, which are described as *righteous* (Matt. 25:37, 46), from the goats, is mercy. The merciful inherit "the kingdom" (Matt. 25:34) and go into "eternal life" (Matt. 25:46). Mercy is an essential ingredient to surpassing righteousness.

Outside of the gospels we see the same thing: "This is how we know who the children of God are and who the children of the devil are: Anyone who *does not practice righteousness* is not a child of God; nor is anyone who *does not love* his brother" (1 John 3:10). Note that not practicing righteousness is the same as not loving. Therefore practicing righteousness involves showing love and mercy.

In examining what Jesus says immediately following his comment on surpassing righteousness he speaks of reconciliation and relationships (Matt. 5:21–26); adultery, lust, and marriage (Matt 5:27–32); integrity (Matt. 5:33–37); vengeance (Matt. 5:38–42); and loving your enemies (Matt. 5:43–47). All of these commands involve love and mercy. Ultimately, of course, all commands come under the umbrella of love, for Paul says, "The commandments, 'Do not commit adultery' . . . and whatever other commandment there may be, are summed up in this one rule: 'Love your neighbor as yourself'" (Rom. 13:9).

Jesus' last command summarizes his concern: "Be perfect, therefore, as your heavenly Father is perfect" (Matt. 5:48). This is often thought to mean that Jesus is commanding sinless perfection. It makes much more sense, however, to understand the call to perfection as a call to love and mercy. We are to love our enemies, for example, as God loves his and "causes his sun to rise on the evil and the good, and sends rain on the righteous and the unrighteous" (Matt. 5:45). We are therefore to be perfect in loving others as our heavenly Father is perfect in loving others. This is confirmed by Luke's version of this verse: "Be merciful, just as your Father is merciful" (Luke 6:36). This is also the intent behind Ephesians 5:1–2: "Be imitators of God . . . and live a life of love." How do we imitate God? Not by being sinless, but by living a life of love.

I said earlier that God's will is expressed in every one of his commands. Now I have said that it is essentially expressed in qualities like mercy and love. Is this a contradiction? Absolutely not. Jesus said that "*All* the Law and the Prophets hang on these two commandments"—love God and love your neighbor (Matt. 22:37–40). Paul said that whoever "loves his fellowman has fulfilled the law . . . Therefore love is the fulfillment of the law" (Rom. 13:8, 10). According to James, the "royal law found in Scripture" is "love your neighbor as yourself" (James 2:8). Whichever way we look at it, surpassing righteousness and doing the Father's will fundamentally consist of love and mercy through and through.

SINNERS BECOME RIGHTEOUS

Jesus requires surpassing righteousness in order to enter heaven (Matt. 5:20). The seriousness behind these words can scarcely be avoided. It is only the "*righteous* man" who will be rewarded (Matt. 10:41). At the end of the age "the angels will come and separate the wicked from the *righteous*" (Matt. 13:49) and "then the *righteous* will shine like the sun in the kingdom of their Father" (Matt. 13:43). It is not the "resurrection of sinners" but the "resurrection of the *righteous*" (Luke 14:14). All these passages point to one thing; only "the *righteous*" will enter in "to eternal life" (Matt. 25:46).

Remember, however, who it is that Jesus calls to follow him. It is not the righteous but sinners. "I have not come to call the righteous, but sinners" (Matt. 9:13; Mark 2:17). Only sinners recognize their need to repent (Luke 5:32). It is only the sick who know they need a doctor. Those who are repentant recognize they have no righteousness of their own, therefore they "hunger and thirst for" what they don't have (Matt. 5:6). "The way of righteousness" was shown to those who are righteous, but they would not believe it. "The tax collectors and the prostitutes" believed, however (Matt. 21:32). They are therefore "entering the kingdom of God ahead of" the Pharisees and the teachers of the law (Matt. 21:31). We might say that they are *surpassing* them.

So be sure to get the order right: sinners are called first. They are sick and need a doctor. However, over the course of time those who were called as sinners are transformed into righteous—not sinless—people.

FIGURE 6: SINNERS BECOME RIGHTEOUS

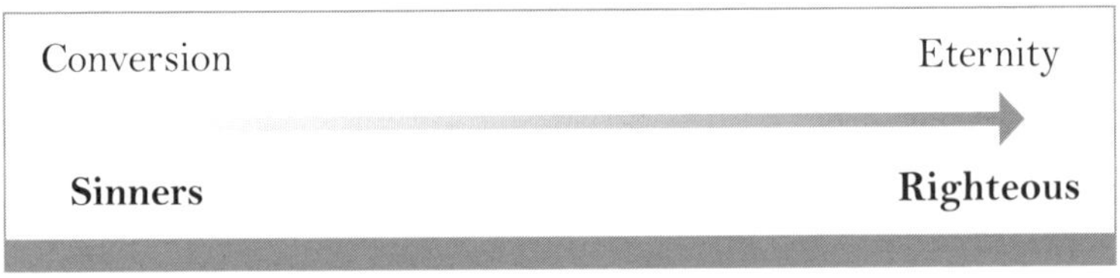

Conversion	Eternity
Sinners	**Righteous**

We see the same thing in Paul. "God . . . justifies the *wicked*" (Rom. 4:5); "While we were still *sinners,* Christ died for us" (Rom. 5:8). "God . . . made us alive with Christ even when we were dead in *transgressions*" (Eph. 2:4–5). It is not, however, the wicked or sinners who inherit the kingdom. "Do you not know that the *wicked* will not inherit the kingdom of God?" (1 Cor. 6:9). Those who live according to "the *sinful* nature . . . will not inherit the kingdom of God" (Gal. 5:18, 21).

I began this chapter by citing some findings by George Barna concerning the incongruity between peoples' faith in God and their lifestyle. Yet a small minority, 7 percent, did not demonstrate such inconsistency. Barna writes, "Christian evangelicals . . . are the group whose faith is most clearly evident in their behavioral choices. . . . Evangelicals emerged as the group most likely to . . . discuss spiritual matters with other people . . . stop watching a television program because of its values or viewpoints. . . . Evangelicals were also distinguished by being the segment least likely to engage in . . . pornographic media . . . their horoscope," and so on.

> Evangelicals also emerged as the group most likely to attend church; pray to God; and read the Bible. By definition, they believe in the accuracy of the Bible, contend that they have a personal responsibility to share their faith with others, claim that their religious faith is very important in their life, reject the idea that Jesus Christ sinned, describe God as the Creator who still rules the universe today, and believe that Satan is real. That body of beliefs—and the worldview it represents—has produced a distinct way of living in an increasingly postmodern culture—a lifestyle that is increasingly at odds with the accepted norms.[8]

A city on a hill cannot be hidden!

---

8. http://www.barna.org/FlexPage.aspx?Page=BarnaUpdate&BarnaUpdateID=16 4 (accessed 10:05PM, December 1, 2006).

CHAPTER SIX

CAN I BE SAVED AND NOT LOVE OTHERS?

Wouldn't church be a great place if it weren't for the people? Just imagine all the things *you* could do. *You* could do everything the way *you* wanted it. *You* could sing the songs *you* liked. *You* could have church go for as long or short as *you* wanted. *You* could adopt a style of worship that suited *you*. There'd be no meetings, no committees, no one holding up the process because they didn't like *your* idea. Of course there would also be no one, except of course *you*!

I'm sure we've all seen incidents among Christians that cause us to raise our eyebrows and scratch our heads. One of the lines brought to mind is, "I don't have to like you, I just have to love you." I've heard Christians say, "I can forgive, but I will never forget." When I went through seminary, I heard about a couple of guys who got into a fight after class over *sanctification*. My brother-in-law, who plays the drums in church, was once told that drums were an instrument of the devil. I remember being scolded years ago by an elderly lady for forgetting to put on the morning tea after church. And on and on we could go.

People, they're pretty hard to escape. God knows this. You only need to examine the "one another" commands in the Bible to see that we are not meant to escape them. Of course I'm not suggesting that I've never done anything that would make people raise their eyebrows and scratch their heads. All of us have our faults and demonstrate them from time to time. Yet my relationship with Christ does not mean I give up all earthly relationships—regardless of how flawed they may be. When we become Christians we become part of a family; we are all now brothers and sisters. We become a member of Christ's *body*. If one part of the body weeps we all weep, and if one part of the body rejoices we all rejoice. We're interconnected.

A few years ago I got a rather big blister on my toe. Rather naively I neglected my toe—after all it was just an unimportant middle toe. Because of my neglect, though, the blister popped, became infected, spread up my leg and made it difficult to walk. Then it gave me a rather high fever and a swollen lymph node in my groin. I should have taken better care of my toe! Just as the parts of our body are bound together, so it is in the body of Christ. We should take care of each other.

This chapter is all about people, specifically how we get on with them and treat them. In Chapter Five we saw that love and mercy are central to surpassing righteousness (Matt. 5:20) and the Father's will (Matt. 7:21). In this chapter we will look more closely at Jesus' teaching on love and mercy and ask the question, "Can I be saved and not show love and mercy toward others?"

ANGER AND RELATIONSHIPS

The seventh beatitude says, "Blessed are the peacemakers, for they will be called sons of God" (Matt. 5:9). Matthew 5:21–26 picks this up.

> You have heard that it was said to the people long ago, "Do not murder, and anyone who murders will be subject to judgment."

I tell you that anyone who is angry with his brother will be subject to judgment. Again, anyone who says to his brother, "Raca," is answerable to the Sanhedrin. But anyone who says, "You fool!" will be in danger of the fire of hell (Matt. 5:21–22).

All murder begins with anger for "from within, out of men's hearts, come . . . murder" (Mark 7:21). We should always deal with our anger.

Cain's Anger

Cain did not deal with his anger, and murder was the result; the problem went deeper than simply anger. It started when Cain offered a lesser sacrifice to God than his brother Abel (Gen. 4:4–5). Hebrews 11:4 tells us that "Abel offered God a better sacrifice than Cain did" because he trusted God and was therefore "commended as a righteous man." The implication is that Cain offered an inferior sacrifice because he did not trust God. And so Cain became "very angry, and his face was downcast" (Gen. 4:5). God challenged Cain to "do what is right" and "master" sin (Gen. 4:7), but Cain did not listen to God due to his lack of trust. It was only a matter of time before his anger got the better of him and Cain killed his brother (Gen. 4:8). Cain's "actions were evil" because he did not trust God. Abel's actions "were righteous" because he did trust God (1 John 3:12).[1]

Here's the point: anger and murder are the outcomes of a failure to trust God. "This is how we know . . . who the children of the devil are . . . anyone who does not love his brother" (1 John 3:10).

---

1. Cf. Colin G. Kruse, *The Letters of John,* Pillar New Testament Commentary, ed. D. A. Carson (Grand Rapids: Eerdmans, 2000), 133–34.

Deal With Anger Quickly

Because murder always begins with anger, it is important to deal with anger quickly. "Therefore, if you are offering your gift at the altar and there remember that your brother has something against you, leave your gift there in front of the altar. First go and be reconciled to your brother; then come and offer your gift" (Matt. 5:23–24). Worship ("offering your gift at the altar") is a waste of time if someone has something against us. We are to take the initiative and go to them lest they flare up in anger.

Angry People In Hell

This brings us to the serious warning. "Anyone who is angry with his brother will be subject to judgment." This includes first, being "answerable to the Sanhedrin," and second, "in danger of the fire of hell" (Matt 5:22). Is Jesus suggesting an earthly judgment *and* an eternal judgment? Probably not. The term "Sanhedrin" is the word "council" in Greek and therefore may refer to God's heavenly council. Regardless, Jesus' words need to be read in light of Matthew 5:20: "unless your righteousness surpasses that of the Pharisees and the teachers of the law, you will certainly not enter the kingdom of heaven." James, who often draws on the Sermon on the Mount, says that "man's anger does not bring about the righteous life that God desires" (James 1:20). Anger is contrary to surpassing righteousness, and those who do not deal with it will not enter the kingdom of heaven. Where then will they go? They will go to the "fire of hell" where "[they] will not get out until [they] have paid the last penny" (Matt. 5:26). But hell's debt is insatiable.

But I Get Angry!

"But I struggle with anger," you say. Jesus' point is not to condemn momentary anger—though this is not to say that momentary anger is always okay. But we all sin, otherwise we would not be urged to mourn over our sin (Matt. 5:4). We must bear in mind that *unresolved* and therefore *unrepentant* anger is the problem here. Those "in danger of the fire of hell" are those who do not confess their anger and mourn over it before God. They do not trust in God or seek him for change. They do not actively pursue peace and mercy in their relationships with others (Matt. 5:3–9).

Reconciliation is always the goal. "If it is possible, as far as it depends on you, live at peace with everyone" (Rom. 12:18). It may not always be possible. The other person may reject your attempt at reconciliation. It should be sought, however, "as far as it depends on you." This means that if the other person won't apologize, my first goal should be maintaining peace between us. Even if the other person refuses to see my side, my first goal is peace. Even if it means I live the rest of my life having been wronged, my first goal is peace.

The point is that we must "settle matters quickly" (Matt. 5:25). I remember having an argument with my wife, then proceeding to spend some time in prayer. I couldn't even begin praying without Jesus' words going through my mind. Imagine it: there I was telling God how much I loved him, yet I was not reconciled with my wife. I might as well have been praying to a brick wall (see 1 Pet. 3:7).

The issue is not so much that of broken relationships. Think of Abraham and Lot (Gen. 13:5–9), Jacob and Esau (Gen. 27; 33), Joseph and his brothers (Gen. 37; 45), Paul and Barnabas (Acts 15:36–41; 2 Tim. 4:11). But what do we do once the relationship is broken? Do we seek reconciliation, and quickly? For "how good and pleasant it is when brothers live together in unity! . . . For there the Lord bestows his blessing, even life forevermore" (Ps. 133:1, 3).

Lust and Sin

Jesus says in the sixth beatitude, "Blessed are the pure in heart, for they will see God" (Matt. 5:8). This is the subject of Matthew 5:27–30:

> You have heard that it was said, 'Do not commit adultery.' But I tell you that anyone who looks at a woman lustfully has already committed adultery with her in his heart. If your right eye causes you to sin, gouge it out and throw it away. It is better for you to lose one part of your body than for your whole body to be thrown into hell. And if your right hand causes you to sin, cut it off and throw it away. It is better for you to lose one part of your body than for your whole body to go into hell (see also Matt. 18:8–9; Mark 9:43, 45, 47–48).

Adultery, Lust—There's No Difference

In Jesus' day adultery (extra-marital sex) was a sin punishable by death. Some Pharisees, for example, brought a woman who had been caught in the act of adultery to Jesus. They wanted to stone her in accordance with Mosaic law (John 8:3–5). Things are similar today in some parts of the world, especially in religious circles. In 2002 in Nigeria a thirty-year-old mother of three was nearly stoned to death for committing adultery[2]. Turkey has made adultery a criminal offense.[3] In 1995 a pastor in America preached a sermon entitled, "Why Adulterous Pastors Should Not Be Restored."[4]

Most of us would probably agree that immorality of any sort is

---

2. (http://aegeantimes.net/index.php?name=News&file=article&sid=1050, (accessed June 22, 2007).
3. http://aegeantimes.net/index.php?name=News&file=article&sid=1050 (accessed June 22, 2007).
4. http://independencebaptist.org/Articles_by_Pastor_Wayne_Reynolds/why_adulterous_pastors_should_not_be_restored.htm (accessed June 22, 2007).

unacceptable. No doubt you'd be horrified if I told you I walked into a person's yard at night and peeped through the window to watch a woman get undressed. You might well label me a pervert. What would you say, however, if I told you that I saw the same scene of a lady getting undressed on television? Why has something so immoral become so acceptable just because it gets viewed through a television screen and not a bedroom window?[5] Jesus says that when we lust in our hearts, we are guilty of committing adultery. This is true whether the medium is a television or a window.

The sin that Jesus equates with adultery here is not mere attraction to the opposite sex. The Greek text reads, "Anyone who looks at a woman *for the purpose* of desiring her." In other words, intentionally using the eyes for lust is adultery.

Radical Action Called For

Jesus tells us that the way to deal with sin is to dismember our eye or hand, anything that causes us to sin (Matt. 5:29a, 30a). We must do anything we can to eradicate whatever tempts us to sin. This strong word is not to be taken literally; even if I gouge out my right eye I can still lust with my left eye. Even lacking both eyes, I still have my mind.

It is significant that Jesus mentions the *right* eye and the *right* hand. Commentators often point out the significance of the right side in the Bible. God spread out the heavens with his "right hand" (Isa. 48:13). He holds us by *our* right hand (Ps. 73:23). Jesus sits at God's "right hand" (Eph. 1:20). The apostles gave Paul and Barnabas the "right hand of fellowship" (Gal. 2:9). The right side is always significant. Even in our culture, the right hand or foot is generally the most active or favored. The same was true in Bible

---

5. Randy Alcorn, *The Purity Principle: God's Safeguards for Life's Dangerous Trails* (Sisters, OR: Multnomah, 2003), 61–62.

times. We should not miss the point—we are to get rid of anything that causes us to sin; this may mean sacrificing our favored things or activities.

So the question is this: what causes you to lust? It may be television, music, internet, magazines around the house, going to the beach, etc. How must we respond? Get rid of it or at least put controls in place. I got rid of our television for this very reason.[6] There's nothing virtuous or legalistic about this. I simply think it's in line with what Jesus says about things that cause sin.

Of course we don't have to think only of lust. Jesus applies this teaching in Matthew 18 to refer to sin in general.

> I tell you the truth, unless you change and become like little children, you will never enter the kingdom of heaven. . . . If your hand or your foot causes you to sin, cut it off and throw it away. It is better for you to enter life maimed or crippled than to have two hands or two feet and be thrown into eternal fire. And if your eye causes you to sin, gouge it out and throw it away. It is better for you to enter life with one eye than to have two eyes and be thrown into the fire of hell (Matt. 18:3, 8–9).

In order to enter the kingdom we must "change and become like children." We are to turn by humbling ourselves (Matt. 18:4). This will involve taking decisive action concerning things that cause us to sin. I don't think we take this seriously enough. We need to be urgent about things that tempt us. Maybe going into a certain shop causes you to be greedy. Perhaps going to bed late causes you to wake up angry, or taking Sunday drives around a certain area of town causes you to covet. Whatever it is, Jesus says—"Get rid of it!" "Do

---

6. Actually after more than a year without a TV someone heard that we didn't have one and insisted that we have there one they weren't using. Nevertheless getting rid of it did the trick to wean me off the need to ever watch it again.

whatever it takes!" Don Carson writes, "We are to deal drastically with sin. We must not pamper it, flirt with it, enjoy nibbling a little of it around the edges."[7] We are to hate it, crush it, dig it out. We must take sin seriously.

Dillydallying is Deadly

The reason for such decisive action is that "it is better for you to lose one part of your body than for your whole body to be thrown into hell" (Matt. 5:29b, 30b). These words are self explanatory; you don't need me to tell you what they mean: *You're going to hell if you don't deal with sin.* It is better to sacrifice cherished things that cause us to sin, making it to heaven's shores, rather than to enjoy momentary toxic pleasures here and spend our existence in the wastelands of hell.

Do we take this seriously? Do we understand that failure to radically deal with our sin is eternally deadly? Once after hearing me speak on lust, someone went home and told his wife, tongue in cheek, "I'm going to hell!" What struck me was the complete lack of seriousness and urgency that he felt. Doubtless he thought that because he was already a Christian this warning could not apply to him. What then, I ask, are we to do with this warning if it does not apply to us? Christians take sin seriously. We don't think that just because we "believe" we'll be okay. It's the unbeliever who doesn't take sin seriously.

Jesus said to some "Jews who had believed him . . . everyone who sins is a slave to sin . . . [and] a slave has no permanent place in the family" (John 8:31, 34). Paul said, "If you live according to the sinful nature, you will die; but if by the Spirit you put to death the misdeeds of the body, you will live" (Rom. 8:13). Please, "Do not be

---

7. D. A. Carson, *The Sermon on the Mount: An Exposition of Matthew 5–7*, Biblical Classics Library (Carlisle, UK: Paternoster, 1994), 49.

deceived: Neither the sexually immoral . . . will inherit the kingdom of God" (1 Cor. 6:9, 10). If we wish to play with sin we play with fire. "Dillydallying is deadly."[8]

John Piper writes concerning lust, "Fix your eyes on Jesus. . . . Be brutal. Hold the promise of Christ before your eyes. Hold it. Hold it! Don't let it go! Keep holding it! How long? As long as it takes. Fight! For Christ's sake, fight till you win! If an electric garage door were about to crush your child, you would hold it up with all your might and holler for help, and hold it and hold it and hold it and hold it. More is at stake, Jesus said, in the habit of lust."[9]

LOVING YOUR ENEMIES

Jesus begins an address to his audience, "You have heard that it was said. . . ." In this instance he does not cite an Old Testament text but what appears to be an incorrect religious interpretation of Leviticus 19:18 (which reads, "Do not seek revenge or bear a grudge against one of your people, but love your neighbor as yourself"): "Love your neighbor and hate your enemy" (Matt. 5:43). Jesus corrects their interpretation: "But I tell you: Love your enemies and pray for those who persecute you" (Matt. 5:44). One is to love, not hate, one's enemy.

It's natural when we think of enemies to think of those who blatantly oppose us. However, the example to love our enemies comes from God himself who "causes his sun to rise on the evil and the good" (Matt. 5:45). Evil people may blatantly oppose us (e.g., Matt. 5:39), or they might be people we consistently don't get along

---

8. William Hendriksen, *The Gospel of Mark,* New Testament Commentary (Grand Rapids: Baker, 1975), 365.
9. John Piper, *Pierced By The Word: Thirty-One Meditations for Your Soul* (Sisters, OR: Multnomah, 2003), 109.

with at work or school; they could also be garden-variety unbelievers (e.g., Matt. 13:49; 22:10).

What Is Love?

How are we to love these people? First, we are to pray for them (Matt. 5:44). We are to pray for their good (see Matt. 5:39–42), which ultimately means (in the case of unbelievers) praying for their salvation (Matt. 5:16).

Second, we are to provide practically for their needs. God provides what his enemies need, sunshine and rain. We should not think that God is doing this just because he's nice. The reason he provides in this way is the same reason he created the world to live in, that is, that we might all seek him and find him (Ps. 19:1–6; Rom. 1:20; Acts 17:26–27); that we might see his glory (Ps. 19:1), living in a reconciled and healthy state. Helping people is only loving when the help points them on toward God and his Son.

Third, we are to meet with our enemies, always holding out hope for reconciliation. It's so tempting to avoid those whom we don't get on with. Yet "if you greet only your brothers, what are you doing more than others? Do not even pagans do that?" (Matt. 5:47).

God himself is our example. Not only does he send sun and rain on everyone, but he "demonstrates his own love for us in this: while we were still *sinners*, Christ died for us," and "when we were God's *enemies*, we were reconciled to him through the death of his Son" (Rom. 5:8, 10). We were once God's enemies, but even then he loved us.

Not Loving Our Enemies

When we do not follow God's example we are no different than any unbeliever (Matt. 5:46–47). So "what reward will you get?" (Matt. 5:46). The answer is "none!" But what reward would we miss out on? The last beatitude provides the answer: the persecuted are to "Rejoice and be glad because great is your *reward* in heaven" (Matt. 5:12). What is their reward? Would it be anything more than the promises already given in the beatitudes—comfort, the earth, filled with righteousness, mercy, seeing God, being called sons of God, in short, the kingdom of heaven (Matt. 5:3–10)? What then is this reward? It is to be "in the presence of God . . . an experience every Christian will enjoy."[10] Therefore the one "who does not love his enemy will not enter into the kingdom of God."[11]

Like Father, Like Son

When we love like God loves we demonstrate that we are his children (Matt. 5:45)—as the adage goes, "like Father, like Son." For this reason Jesus says, "All men will know that you are my disciples, if you love one another" (John 13:35). Without love we cast doubt upon our salvation to the unbeliever. But when we love our enemies, the "reward will be great, and you will be sons of the Most High" (Luke 6:35).

BEING JUDGMENTAL

It's so easy to become proud of our righteousness. Jesus anticipates the danger and so his first words in Matthew 7 are, "Do not judge, or you too will be judged" (Matt. 7:1; see also Luke 6:37).

---

10. David K. Lowery, "A Theology of Matthew" in *A Biblical Theology of the New Testament*, ed. Roy B. Zuck and Darrell L. Bock (Chicago: Moody, 1994), 63.
11. John Piper, *"Love Your Enemies": Jesus' Love Command in the Synoptic Gospels and in the Early Christian Paraenesis*, Society for New Testament Studies Monograph Series, ed. R. McL. Wilson and M. E. Thrall, vol. 38 (Cambridge: Cambridge University Press, 1979), 60–61.

Do Not Judge What?

But what does it mean not to judge? It cannot mean never confronting another Christian about their sin (see Matt. 18:15–17); Paul rebukes the Christians at Corinth for not judging a man caught in gross sin: "Are you not to *judge* those inside [the church]?" (1 Cor. 15:12). James says that if we bring a person back from sin we save his soul from eternal death (James 5:19–20). How many people may not be in heaven because we believed we should never judge?

What then are we meant to judge? James is helpful here. "Brothers, do not slander one another. Anyone who *speaks against his brother* or *judges him* speaks against the law and judges it" (James 4:11). We are not to speak "against" another person. This means we are not to talk about anyone in such a way that would tarnish their reputation. We are to avoid judgments even when they may be true and verifiable. R. Kent Hughes, in his excellent book *Disciplines of a Godly Man,* writes, "most people think it is okay to convey negative information if it is true. . . . It seems almost a moral responsibility! By such reasoning, criticism behind another's back is thought to be all right as long as it is based on fact. Likewise, denigrating gossip (of course it is never called gossip!) is seen as okay if the information is true. Thus many believers use truth as a license to righteously diminish others' reputations."[12]

Why We Shouldn't Judge

Jesus gives the reason for not judging: "You too will be judged. For in the same way you judge others, you will be judged, and with the measure you use, it will be measured to you" (Matt. 7:1b–2). Some think that this means the judgmental person will get a taste of

---

12. R. Kent Hughes, *Disciplines of a Godly Man* (Wheaton: Crossway, 2001), 140–41.

their own medicine. Life has a way of making sure we reap what we sow. However, it is clear that eternal judgment is in view.

Jesus labels the judgmental person a "hypocrite" (Matt. 7:5). The hypocrite is one who has received his "reward in full" (Matt. 6:2, 5, 16). That means he or she will receive no eternal reward, or in other words, will be far from God's presence. For this reason hypocrites will hear the words, "Away from me" (Matt. 7:23). They will be excluded from God's kingdom (Matt. 23:13) since their graceless attitudes toward others did not constitute the surpassing righteousness required to enter the kingdom. They are "son[s] of hell" (Matt. 23:15) and they will be assigned "a place with the hypocrites, where there will be weeping and gnashing of teeth" (Matt. 24:51).

We must take this warning seriously. No one can believe in Jesus Christ and embrace God's forgiveness, mercy, and grace yet not show it to others. Such a person has never truly grasped the gospel. One cannot believe the gospel yet not live it. This is not to say that we will be perfect, but it *is* to say that we will recognize our judgmental attitudes and mourn, hungering and thirsting for righteousness. Regardless of what we say we believe, if we engage in merciless slander we need to take stock: "judgment without mercy will be shown to anyone who has not been merciful" (James 2:12–13).

How Can We Stop Judging?

To purge ourselves of judgmental behavior we must remember that we are part of a family. Jesus uses the term "brother" three times in this passage (Matt. 7:3–5). We must understand that when we judge other Christians we are judging a *brother* or *sister* in Christ, another family member. In my biological family I love my sister. Growing up it did not seem that way; we certainly had our fights. But I'm older now, and I am wholly interested in her well being. I am genuinely glad when things go well for her and genuinely sad when they don't. How much more should this be the case in our spiritual family? We are brothers and sisters; we should be concerned for each others' spiritual welfare. "Therefore, let us stop passing judgment on one another. Instead, make up your mind not to put any stumbling block or obstacle in your *brother's* way" (Rom. 14:13).

We must also examine ourselves: "First take the plank out of your own eye" (Matt. 7:5a). We would be slower to judge if we first looked at the planks in our own lives. Furthermore, "if we judged ourselves, we would not come under judgment" (1 Cor. 11:31).

Having examined yourselves, "then you will see clearly to remove the speck from your brother's eye" (Matt. 7:5b). Imagine if my wife came to me with a speck of dust in her eye. What would be the "family" thing to do? Would it be to say, "Just a minute, I'll get to it after I first check the oil in the car, mow the lawn, fix the plumbing," and then, without washing my hands, take the speck out? No, the *family* thing to do would be to gently and lovingly take that speck out. Specks in the eye are most uncomfortable. They hinder everything we do. We can't concentrate. What we need is for someone to care enough about us to gently remove the speck so we can get on with things. "*Brothers*, if someone is caught in a sin, you who are spiritual [i.e., having no plank] should restore him *gently*" (Gal. 6:1).

Forgiveness

"For if you forgive men when they sin against you, your heavenly Father will also forgive you. But if you do not forgive men their sins, your Father will not forgive your sins" (Matt. 6:14–15; see also Mark 11:25).

Who of us has not felt uncomfortable reading these words? God's forgiveness is dependent upon our forgiveness of others! "What? That's not fair. Isn't God's love and forgiveness unconditional? You don't realize what so-and-so did to me. I just can't forgive them. I won't forgive them. So am I still a Christian? Will I go to heaven when I die?"

The answer to these questions is not immediately obvious from what Jesus says here. In another context, though, Jesus gives a parable that makes these words painfully clear.

Why Forgive?—A Parable

The parable arises as a result of a question from Peter over something Jesus had said. "If your brother sins against you, go and show him his fault, just between the two of you" (Matt. 18:15). Peter later asks, "Lord, how many times shall I forgive my brother when he sins against me? Up to seven times?" (Matt. 18:21). Jesus tells Peter to go higher: "not seven times, but seventy times seven" (Matt. 18:22). Jesus doesn't mean stop forgiving at 490 times. Forgiveness is to be unlimited. It doesn't matter how many times someone sins against you; forgive them every time. Jesus then gives a parable to explain why we should forgive so readily and generously.

First of all, the parable is about the "kingdom of heaven" (Matt. 18:23), of which we know that no one without surpassing righteousness will enter (Matt. 5:20). The basic details are that a servant owed his king an astronomical sum of money—"ten thousand talents" (Matt. 18:24). Actually, the sum owed is more like a zillion talents (in Greek, literally "myriads of talents"), which is a lot of money in any day; millions, perhaps billions of dollars. He is brought before the king who wants to collect his money, but the servant cannot possibly repay.

The king therefore orders that the servant's entire family be sold into slavery along with their possessions. The money from the sale would contribute to repaying the debt. But top price for a slave fetches about one talent, so even a large family would fetch only a few talents—a long way from a zillion! The servant's situation is utterly hopeless. There's no way in the world he can repay the debt. So he does what any man or women in his situation would do. He begs for mercy: "Be patient with me . . . and I will pay back everything" (Matt. 18:26). People in desperate situations will, of course, make promises that they know they can never fulfill; anything to buy some time. The servant could never pay back everything, and he would know it. Nevertheless, the king goes beyond what is asked and responds with compassion. He cancels the whole debt, the entire zillion talents, and lets the servant go. Can you imagine the servant's relief?

This now free and *relieved* servant walks outside, and "he found one of his fellow servants who owed him a hundred denarii" (Matt. 18:28)—one hundred days wages; a fair amount, but if you consider that six thousand denarii equals just one talent, one hundred denarii is a drop in the ocean. If the first servant owed billions of dollars, the second servant owed a few cents. What happens next is absolutely unbelievable.

The first servant doesn't even wait to find out if the other man is able to pay and immediately resorts to violence: "He grabbed him and began to choke him. 'Pay back what you owe me!' he demanded" (Matt. 18:28). This servant also falls to his hands and knees and begs for mercy: "Be patient with me, and I will pay you back" (Matt. 18:29). Having himself just said these exact words to the king, the first servant could not have possibly forgotten his own helpless situation just a few moments ago.

Yet "he refused. Instead, he went off and had the man thrown into prison until he could pay the debt" (Matt. 18:30). Unbelievable! Naturally the other servants are horrified and tell the king who calls the first servant and says, "You wicked servant! . . . I canceled all that debt of yours because you begged me to. Shouldn't you have had mercy on your fellow servant just as I had on you?" (see Matt.

18:32–33). Of course he should have had mercy. Can you imagine getting so irate over a few measly cents after having been freed from such an enormous debt? Surely we can appreciate the justice—even if we wince a bit—when the story concludes: "In anger his master turned him over to the jailers to be tortured, until he should pay back all he owed" (Matt. 18:34).

This is How God Will Treat Those Who Do Not Forgive

Jesus now explains the characters of the parable. "This is how my heavenly Father will treat each of you unless you forgive your brother from your heart" (Matt. 18:35). The *king* is God. And so we see in this parable that God is patient, compassionate, and merciful. He releases and forgives people from the enormity of their sin. Whatever else this parable teaches, it does not teach that salvation is earned. Salvation is based on the compassionate and gracious forgiveness of God.

The *servant* who owed a zillion talents represents every person who has been forgiven by God. They have been forgiven a debt they could never repay. Everyone who claims to know Jesus as Savior fits into this category.

The *servant's attitude* toward the other servant who owed one hundred denarii represents those who claim to be Christians yet are unwilling to forgive others who sin against them.

The warning to those who do not forgive other Christians is chilling. God will treat such people in the same way the king treated the unforgiving servant if they do not forgive *from the heart,* which means forgiveness must be sincere. Those who do not forgive will not be forgiven (Matt. 6:15).

But what does it mean that God will not forgive? There is no encouragement in this warning. It can only mean one thing: God will not forgive someone for all eternity, that is, they will be in hell. There are at least two reasons for this.

First, the term "jailers" in Greek is "torturers." The term is used throughout the New Testament to describe people who will be in hell where "they will be tormented ["tortured"] day and night for ever and ever" (Rev. 20:10).

Second, the king calls the unforgiving servant a "wicked servant" (Matt. 18:32). Later on Jesus tells another parable about another "wicked, lazy servant" (Matt. 25:26). This servant is to be thrown "outside, into the darkness, where there will be weeping and gnashing of teeth" (Matt. 25:30)—in other words, hell.

There is no room for the unforgiving person in heaven. If God's character is compassionate, patient, merciful, and forgiving, then those who claim to belong in his kingdom must also demonstrate these same qualities. We cannot claim to embrace God's splendid mercy and forgiveness yet not show that same mercy and forgiveness to others.

> After what God in Christ has done for us, could we ever refuse to make any attempt to forgive those who have sinned against us? I believe the point of Jesus' parable of the unforgiving servant, as harsh as it may sound, is that the answer to that question is "no," for no one who has truly sensed how much he has owed God, how much she has offended God, how much his sin has separated him from an infinitely holy and loving creator, and who also recognizes that God in Christ has forgiven her, through no merit of her own—no one who truly understands these concepts and thus has received and appropriated that forgiveness could ever act in such a way as the servant in this parable. True Christians could never absolutely refuse to forgive one another, choosing instead to inflict the worst possible vengeance.[13]

---

13. Craig L. Blomberg, *Preaching the Parables: From Responsible Interpretation to Powerful Proclamation* (Grand Rapids: Baker, 2004), 77.

The Struggle To Forgive

Does this parable say anything about whether one can lose their salvation? It certainly doesn't teach that anyone can *earn* their salvation. Its point is simply that those who do not forgive will not be saved—that is, admitted into heaven.

Do you fit into this category? Is there someone right now you are not forgiving? We're not at liberty to take this warning lightly and think it couldn't possibly apply to us. A pastor and friend recently told me of a husband and wife he had been counseling. My friend pointed out a text of the Bible to them to shed some light on their situation to which the wife replied, "I don't like that verse." That's not taking Scripture seriously. This warning applies to *you* and to *me*, even if you or I won't forgive others.

I need to stress again, however, that the person Jesus has in mind here is the person who shows no desire to forgive and remains unrepentant in spite of forgiveness—not that this makes occasional un-forgiveness okay. Craig Blomberg sensitively notes: "I'm not talking about somebody who struggles to forgive others but keeps on trying. I'm not talking about someone who knows he or she needs to forgive, even wants to, but finds it very, very difficult.... What I am talking about is an attitude that doesn't even care, that refuses even to try to forgive."[14]

REMEMBER, "BLESSED ARE THE POOR IN SPIRIT"

Do you now feel helpless and inadequate? Join the club. Who is able to do what Jesus demands? No one! Remember the very first verse of the Sermon on the Mount, "blessed are the poor in spirit" (Matt. 5:3). The kingdom belongs to the humble, not to those who think they have the ability. We may as well try and push a camel

---

14. Ibid., 113.

through a needle's eye. Obedience to Jesus' commands only comes as we depend completely upon God and hunger and thirst for his righteousness. The answer is never within me; it's always in Christ, and we must come back time and time again to Jesus' beatitudes to remember this. This lifestyle relies on utter dependence on the empowerment of the Holy Spirit, especially when you take into account the end of Jesus' message: "Everyone who hears these words of mine and does not put them into practice is like a foolish man who built his house on sand . . . the winds blew and beat against that house, and it fell with a great crash" (Matt. 7:26–27). We must depend upon God's enabling grace for the ability to put his words into practice.

THE GOOD SAMARITAN: MERCY IN ACTION

The parable of the Good Samaritan arises from a discussion with Jesus and an "expert in the law." His field of expertise is Old Testament law. He questions Jesus, not looking for information—he knows it all already—but "to test Jesus." His question is, "What must I do to inherit eternal life?" (Luke 10:25).

Question: How Do I Get Eternal Life?

The Greek phrase *zôên aiônion* ("eternal life") occurs once in the Old Testament in Daniel. After a time of unprecedented distress God's people "will be delivered. Multitudes who sleep in the dust of the earth will awake: some to *everlasting life* (*zôên aiônion*), others to shame and everlasting contempt" (Dan. 12:1–2). Eternal life here is a reference to the end of the age when the righteous will be resurrected. This became standard Jewish belief among some Jews, including the Pharisees.

It is against this backdrop that the lawyer asks, "What must I do to have everlasting life at the resurrection?" or "What must I do to get into heaven?" Jesus asks the expert what he thinks (Luke 10:26). The lawyer cites Deuteronomy 6:5 ("Love the Lord your God with all your heart and with all your soul and with all your strength and with all your mind") and Leviticus 19:18 ("Love your neighbor as yourself") as his answer (Luke 10:27).

Answer: "Do This and You Will Live"

"You have answered correctly," Jesus replied. "Do this and you will live" (Luke 10:28)—"live *eternally*," that is. Now that's an interesting response. We might have expected Jesus to say, "You're right, you need to love God but you don't need to do anything else." As one writer wrestles with it, "*Doing* and *inheriting* are not compatible terms. The gospel is good news freely available. It's not a matter of 'go and do.'"[15] Another has said: "The parable of the Good Samaritan . . . seems to promote a kind of works righteousness worthy of St. James rather than Paul's disciple Luke. Its punch lines . . . both say: 'Go and do!'"[16]

That may be so, but we are still left with Jesus' answer. He does not give the lawyer any indication that he is on the wrong track. In fact he even repeats the command at the end of the parable: "Go and *do* likewise" (Luke 10:37). It is difficult to escape the notion that the lawyer must indeed *do* something to inherit eternal life. I will address this shortly, but first let's take a look at the parable.

The Explanation: A Parable

It seems that the lawyer did not think that he had a problem with loving God. He was probably much like the Pharisee in another

---

15. Mike Graves, "Luke 10:25–37: The Moral of the 'Good Samaritan,'" *Review and Expositor* 94 (1997), 272.
16. Stephen F. Noll, "The Good Samaritan and Justification by Faith," *Mission and Ministry* 8 (1990), 36.

parable who "stood up and prayed about himself: 'God, I thank you that I am not like other men—robbers, evildoers, adulterers—or even like this tax collector. I fast twice a week and give a tenth of all I get'" (Luke 18:11–12). So his next question does not concern God at all but his neighbor. The lawyer "wanted to justify himself," in other words he wanted to know who he didn't have to love. "So he asked Jesus, 'who is my neighbor?'" (Luke 10:29).

So Jesus answers him with a parable. "A man was going down from Jerusalem to Jericho, when he fell into the hands of robbers. They stripped him of his clothes, beat him and went away, leaving him half dead" (Luke 10:30). Two people separately pass by the wounded man. Both are religious men, a priest and a Levite, and both are returning from worshipping God in Jerusalem (Luke 10:31–32).

These men know the Old Testament law. Doubtless they were unwilling to help since, for all they knew, the victim could have been dead. Leviticus 21:11 states that one "must not enter a place where there is a dead body. He must not make himself unclean."

Then came a Samaritan. But since "Jews do not associate with Samaritans" (John 4:9) no respectable Jew would expect much from one. Yet when the Samaritan "saw him, he took pity on him." Notice how far this pity extends: "He went to him and bandaged his wounds, pouring on oil and wine. Then he put the man on his own donkey, took him to an inn and took care of him." Did he not have other things to do? Was there not some place he had to be—home or a business meeting or something? "The next day he took out two silver coins and gave them to the innkeeper. 'Look after him,' he said, 'and when I return, I will reimburse you for any extra expense you may have'" (Luke 10:33–35). This is genuine mercy. It begins with "pity" and is expressed in very real help. First the immediate needs of cuts and bruises are attended to, then the Samaritan thinks more long term about a bed for the next few nights and the money to pay for it. Every need is met from beginning to end.

Jesus now asks the lawyer, "Which of these three do you think was a neighbor to the man who fell into the hands of robbers?" The man who showed mercy of course. Jesus told him, "Go and do likewise" (Luke 10:36–37). This is completely unexpected. The lawyer wanted to know who is neighbor was. Now Jesus is telling him to *be* a neighbor. The point: a neighbor is not just someone in need but someone who cares for someone in need. *Everyone* then is a neighbor.

True Religion

The parable clearly illustrates the importance of showing mercy to others, but it is easy to forget that the parable is an answer to the question, "What must I do to inherit eternal life?" Here are some observations.

First, the lawyer's question does not concern *conversion* but entrance into heaven. Therefore, when Jesus says, "Do this and you will live," he is not saying what one must do to become a Christian. Rather he is *describing* what a Christian is: that is, someone who loves God and their neighbor.

Second, knowing the Bible is not enough. The priest and the Levite both knew the law, but they failed to do it. Those who "merely listen to the word . . . deceive" themselves (James 1:22). It's not enough to say, "Lord, Lord." We must do the Father's will in order to enter the kingdom of heaven (Matt. 7:21). Obedience without mercy is not godly obedience (Matt. 9:13; 12:7). The Samaritan was an outsider when it came to matters of the law, but he nevertheless put it into practice. This is what counts (Rom 2:12–16, 25–29).

Third, the command to "Do this and you will live" (Luke 10:28) is also a command to love God, not just one's neighbor. Yet Jesus says nothing more about loving God in the parable. All the same, when he repeats the command "Go and do likewise" at the end of the parable, Jesus is still intending the lawyer to "Go love God *and* your neighbor." The lesson then on what it means to love your neighbor is also a lesson on what it means to love God. Jesus may as well have asked, "Which of these three do you think loved God—the priest, the Levite, or the Samaritan?"

If we really love God, that love will show itself in how we treat others. The very religious priest and Levite doubtless claimed to love God with all of their being, however God would say they were liars (1 John 4:20).

The Excuses We Make

During my seminary days I would get up early in the morning to walk and pray. I remember one Saturday morning walking and praying when a tall, thin black man came out from behind a dumpster. He approached me and bits of white bread spilled out from his mouth as he spoke. He wanted money for food. I responded with a shake of the head together with "I'm sorry, no," and continued on my way—praying! As I walked on—praying (!)—it suddenly occurred to me what I had done, and what I was doing *right then*. Was I, a praying seminary student, any different from the priest or Levite? "If anyone has material possessions and sees his brother in need but has no pity on him, how can the love of God be in him?" (1 John 3:17).

When it comes to the subject of loving others, I find that people will invariably come up with all sorts of scenarios. "What if you loan someone one hundred dollars, and he squanders it and then comes back and asks for more? Should I loan him more?" "What if I really don't get along with the person?" "What if they're always coming to me for help?" "What if I'm too busy?" These are all attempts to justify ourselves. We want to know when it's okay not to help people.

We want to "protect" ourselves—our lives, our money, our rights, and our time. And so we *learn* to say "no" and not put ourselves in situations where we might be taken advantage of, saying in effect "I'll be a neighbor when it's safe and convenient." But this is the way that *unbelievers* operate (Matt. 5:46–47). Christians are different. Jesus will not let us justify ourselves.

Jesus is doubtless aware of the dangers of a Samaritan stopping on the Jerusalem-Jericho road to help someone in trouble. Furthermore, the Samaritan didn't seem to have any qualms about time. Surely he needed to be somewhere, and who knows how much money the situation would end up costing him. The inn-keeper might rip him off. All the excuses we might use not to help someone—danger, time, money—Jesus seems to quash. Instead he urges radical, excuse-free, unabashed mercy and says, "Go and do likewise."

Love: The Defining Mark of a Christian

The way we treat others is extremely important—so much so that when we do not treat others in a loving and merciful way it casts doubt upon our salvation. This should not surprise us since our love for others is merely a reflection of our love for God. This is true throughout the New Testament. We can rightly say, therefore, that love is the defining mark of a Christian (see Rom. 12:8–10; 1 Cor. 13:1–3, 13; James 2:8; 1 Pet. 4:8; 2 John 5–6). It is the outworking of everything that is basic to being a Christian: "The only thing that counts is faith expressing itself through love" (Gal. 5:6; cf. 5:13; 1 Pet. 1:22; 1 John 3:23). Love for others is thus an indication that salvation is present: "We know that we have passed from death to life, because we love our brothers" (1 John 3:14; cf. Heb. 6:9–10; 1 John 4:7, 12, 16–17). If our lives are not characterized by genuine love for others, we are not Christians. "This is how we know who the children of God are and who the children of the devil are: Anyone who does not do what is right is not a child of God; nor is anyone who does not love his brother" (1 John 3:10; cf. 3:14, 17; 4:8, 20).

I have just spent the last four days in hospital with my four-year-old son, Luke. The night before this ordeal began, my wife was actually in the hospital with our two-month-old who had to be put on oxygen. It was during this time that Luke became very unwell. At 4:00 AM he said to me, "This is the worst night ever!" For a night and a day, I looked after Luke and cleaned up every conceivable mess. No sooner had I cleaned up one that I was on to another one. I had the washing machine going continuously. Then our three-year-old vomited all over the bathroom—I'd never experienced projectile vomiting until then. Eventually we went to the doctor and from there found ourselves in the emergency room at the hospital. There I sat with Luke for six hours; we were discharged only to be back later that night and eventually admitted. Five days later we were through it. With tears in my eyes I held my son down while doctors and nurses stuck a tube up his nose and down his throat; I laid awake into the early hours of the morning with him; I slept with him five nights running, and the messes continued, of course. I was far more of a nurse to him than the nurses in the hospital.

In the midst of it all, my wife said to me, "You're a good father." Of course, I denied it. But the truth is that there were some moments when I did think to myself, "Boy, I'm a good father." While we were in the hospital I thought a lot about what parents do for their children. I was in the children's ward, and there wasn't one child in there without at least one parent. All of them had come in via the emergency room, and who knows what sacrifices they had all made prior to that point. But that's what parents do for their children.

Someone once asked me whether parenting was a sacrifice. Obviously, they did not have kids. I thought, "What a question!" Of course, it's not a sacrifice because I love my son; that's the way it's been for the last few days during his illness. That's the way it was for all the parents I saw. We all gladly sacrificed ourselves lovingly for our children; we wouldn't even think not to.

But here's the challenge. Jesus said, "If you love those who love you, what reward will you get? Are not even the tax collectors doing that? And if you greet only your brothers, what are you doing more than others? Do not even pagans do that?" (Matt. 5:46–47). Do you see? I may have thought I was a good father in doing what I did for my son. Yet I was doing nothing more than any other parent would do. I was challenged as I spent time in hospital to think about the Samaritan who took pity on a man who was his enemy. What love this Samaritan displayed. He went the extra mile.

Any parent would do for their child what that Samaritan did for this man. But would we do it for others? Would we do it for those who don't like us? Those we don't know? That's *true* love; that's Christian love. That's what sets us apart from unbelievers who simply love those who love them. That's the love Jesus showed us—ungodly sinners. "Go and do likewise."

CHAPTER SEVEN

CAN I BE SAVED AND BE WEALTHY?

Why is it that we don't like to be challenged on what the Bible says about money? Is it because the Bible is so straightforward? It's rather difficult to get around, "You *cannot* serve both God and money" (Matt. 6:24). Or consider what Jesus said to a rich young man, "If you want to be perfect, go, sell your possessions and give to the poor" (Matt. 19:21). "Oh, but this is a command to *one* man," I hear you say. On the contrary, Jesus didn't only say it to one man; he said it to twelve: "Sell your possessions and give to the poor" (Luke 12:33a).

This makes us extremely uncomfortable. How can we take the Bible seriously yet somehow ignore these passages? We must not approach this subject by trying to make sure that we preserve "our opulent [w]estern lifestyle."[1]

I don't think it is a coincidence that Jesus spoke more often on money than any other subject, even heaven and hell itself. If Jesus was preaching in our churches today, he would be speaking seven to eight Sundays a year on money. Why would he devote so much time

---

1. Joseph H. Hellerman, "Wealth and Sacrifice in early Christianity: Revisiting Mark's Presentation of Jesus' Encounter With The Rich Young Ruler," *Trinity Journal* (2000): 143–45.

to money? Could it be that God knows that there is nothing that tugs at our heart, and thus competes with him more, than money? Could it have anything to do with a survey carried out by the Barna Group in 2004 revealing that "Christians are more likely to invest their money in lottery tickets than are non-Christians"?[2]

CAN I LOVE GOD AND MONEY?

Treasures On Earth

> Do not store up for yourselves treasures on earth, where moth and rust destroy, and where thieves break in and steal (Matt. 6:19).

What exactly does it mean to store up treasures on earth? We find the answer in a parable Jesus told about "a certain rich man" whose fields one year produced a bumper crop (Luke 12:16–20). The harvest was so good that the man "thought to himself, 'What shall I do? I have no place to store my crops.'" He chose to demolish his barns and "build bigger ones" then retire, thinking he'd "take life easy; eat, drink and be merry." Yet little did he know that on that very night God would say to him, "You fool! This very night your life will be demanded from you. Then who will get what you have prepared for yourself?"

This parable is an illustration of what it looks like to store up treasure on earth. Jesus says, "This is how it will be with anyone who *stores up* things for himself but is not rich toward God" (Luke 12:21). In the first place Jesus tells the parable to warn people "against all kinds of greed; a man's life does not consist in the abundance of his

---

[2]. http://www.barna.org/FlexPage.aspx?Page=BarnaUpdate&BarnaUpdateID=164 (accessed 9:50pm, December 1, 2006).

possessions" (Luke 12:15). Storing up treasures on earth is essentially greed and based on the false premise that one's life consists of possessions. Notice that the reason the farmer built bigger barns was to prepare for *himself* (Luke 12:20). He believed *his* life consisted in the abundance of wealth rather than the abundance of God.

James warns "rich people" to beware "because of the misery that is coming upon them" because "their wealth has rotted, and *moths* have eaten their clothes. . . . They have *stored up* wealth in the last days" (James 5:1–3, my translation). How so? They have "failed to pay the workmen who mowed [their] fields" their wages (James 5:4). At the expense of others then they "have lived on earth in luxury and self-indulgence" (James 5:5).

Greed, using our surplus on ourselves, luxury at the expense of others, self-indulgence—these are all descriptions of what it means to store up earthly treasures.

Storing Up Treasures in Heaven

> But store up for yourselves treasures in heaven, where moth and rust do not destroy, and where thieves do not break in and steal (Matt. 6:20).

Obviously Jesus is saying that we must be preoccupied with eternal rather than perishable things. We should not worry about earthly things—"your life, what you will eat or drink; or about your body, what you will wear" (Matt. 6:25). Instead we should "seek first his kingdom, and all these things will be given to you as well" (Matt. 6:33).

But what does it mean practically to store up treasures in heaven? What does this look like in my life? Once again Jesus' parable in Luke 12 is instructive. What should this farmer have done with his surplus crop? The answer is given to the disciples, "Sell your possessions and give to the poor. Provide purses for yourselves that will not wear out, *a treasure in heaven* that will not be exhausted, where no thief comes near and no moth destroys" (Luke 12:33).

What is Jesus saying? He's saying we should sell our possessions and give to the poor! (I'm not making this up; that's what the text says!) If we do this, we will provide for ourselves a treasure in heaven that will never perish. It's at this point we are challenged as to whether we take the Bible seriously. The early church took Jesus seriously for they "sold their possessions and goods, they gave to anyone as he had need" (Acts 2:45). As a result "there were no needy persons among them. For from time to time those who owned lands or houses sold them, brought the money from the sales and put it at the apostles' feet, and it was distributed to anyone as he had need" (Acts 4:34–35). Should this surprise us? After all Jesus told his disciples to teach new disciples "to obey everything I have commanded you" (Matt. 28:20). Presumably they did, and we see the results in the early church. Likewise, drawing on language from Acts 2:44, the apostle Paul taught that believers should "*share* with God's people who are in need" (Rom. 12:13). The early church took Jesus seriously and practiced what he preached. Shouldn't we?

But does Jesus mean *all* our possessions? To answer this we need to understand why God "gives [us] the ability to produce wealth" (Deut. 8:18). He has given this ability for two reasons. First, we are *to provide for our family.*

> God's people must learn to devote themselves to doing what is good, in order that they may provide for *daily necessities* (Titus 3:14).

> If anyone does not provide for his relatives, and especially for his *immediate family,* he has denied the faith and is worse than an unbeliever (1 Tim. 5:8).

We are thus responsible to provide for those who are nearest and dearest to us. But there is a second reason that God enables us to make money: *to help those in need.*

> By this kind of hard work we must help *the weak* (Acts 20:35).

> He must work, doing something useful with his own hands, that he may have something to share with *those in need* (Eph. 4:28).

It's very clear. After we have taken care of the livelihood of our own family we are to use what's left, what's surplus, to provide for those in need. The rich fool who built bigger barns to store his surplus was concerned only about himself. He never thought of using his surplus to help the poor. Instead he upgraded. This is a philosophy that pervades the Western world. As we earn more income we upgrade to the next house, car, vacation, dietary level, and so forth. Yet the Bible, and Jesus in particular, is saying that we are not to use our surpluses to advance our earthly lifestyles—after all they're only temporary—but rather to give to the poor and advance the cause of God's kingdom.[3]

How Much Is Enough?

Our minds automatically want to ask the question, what kind of lifestyle is satisfactory? It seems to me that this is something we each must work out before God. I think it's helpful to keep a couple of things in mind as we do so.

First, we need to learn to be content with less for "we brought nothing into the world, and we can take nothing out of it. If we have food and clothing, we will be content" (1 Tim. 6:7). The problem

---

3. My thinking on this originally began with reading John Piper, *Brothers, We Are Not Professionals: A Plea to Pastors for Radical Ministry* (Nashville: Broadman and Holman, 2002), 167–72.

with the farmer is that he believed his life consisted in the alleged satisfaction of his possessions. As Christians, God must be our contentment. We should be able to honestly claim "apart from you I have no good thing" (Ps. 16:2), thus being "content with what [we] have, because God has said, 'Never will I leave you; never will I forsake you'" (Heb. 13:5).

Second, we should not be fooled into thinking that giving large amounts of money while maintaining an extravagant lifestyle is pleasing to God. On one occasion Jesus witnessed "many rich people" giving large amounts, though it was "a poor widow" who gave "all she had to live on" that received praise from Jesus. Those who gave lots of money merely "gave out of their wealth" (Mark 12:43–44). They simply gave what they didn't need to maintain their expensive habits. R. Kent Hughes thus concludes that giving according to New Testament principles "affects one's lifestyle. There are things one cannot have and things foregone when one indulges in grace giving." He goes on to quote C. S. Lewis:

> [I]f our expenditure on comforts, luxuries, amusements, etc., is up to the standard common among those with the same income as our own, we are probably giving away too little. If our charities do not at all pinch or hamper us, I should say they are too small. There ought to be things we should like to do and cannot do because our charitable expenditure excludes them.[4]

For those whose lives consist in the abundance of their possessions, to live this way will seem impossible. But if life is lived out of the abundance of God, we won't regret giving it all away.

Examples of Storing Up Treasures in Heaven

Preacher and hymn writer John Wesley lived in eighteenth century

---

4. R. Kent Hughes, *Disciplines of a Godly Man* (Wheaton: Crossway, 2001), 197.

England and is best known as being one of the major founders of the Methodist movement. Wesley understood very well why God enabled him to earn money. Take a look at his budget:[5]

	Income	Expenses	To the Poor
Year 1	£30	£28	£2
Year 2	£60	£28	£32
Year 3	£90	£28	£62
Year 4	£120	£28	£92
Eventually	£1400+	£30	£1400+

TABLE 2: JOHN WESLEY'S BUDGET

The amounts aren't important. It's no use thinking how remarkable it was to live on twenty-eight pounds a year—it was eighteenth century England!—though we should note that inflation was zero in his day. The point is that Wesley decided on a responsible lifestyle and anything he earned over what was needed to maintain that lifestyle was given away to the poor. This meant that as his income increased he was able to give proportionately more of his income. So much for tithing! What a fine example of storing up treasures in heaven.

A more recent example comes from Denver Seminary professor Craig Blomberg.

> Early in our married life, while living for three years in Scotland . . . fellowshipping with very fiscally frugal, conservative Scottish Baptists . . . my wife and I became convinced that passages like 2 Corinthians

---

5. Quoted in Matt Friedman, *The Accountability Connection* (Wheaton: Victor, 1992), 81.

8:13–15 led logically to . . . a 'graduated tithe.' We began giving 10 percent to the Lord's work while we were living on a shoestring and giving just about all that we earned (and some that we borrowed) to the university in which I was doing my doctoral studies. We trusted that God would increase our annual income above mere cost-of-living increases so that we could then give a higher percentage. We didn't follow any fixed formula but simply committed to increase that percentage as our income grew. After twenty-three years of marriage, our giving, both to our church and to other Christian organizations and individuals who are concerned to meet the holistic needs of people's bodies and spirits, has topped 40 percent of our family's annual gross income.[6]

Blomberg's thoughts actually influenced me by way of another book he wrote (*Neither Poverty nor Riches: A Biblical Theology of Possessions*).[7] I was preaching at the time through Matthew 6:19–34 and, like Blomberg, my wife and I became convinced that the New Testament teaches a graduated tithe. Our giving is now based on surplus money, that is, money that would otherwise be spent on unnecessary or luxury items. We are left over, in theory, with a modest amount to spend on daily necessities. We're not perfect. At times it seems rather subjective. Our income comes from two sources and is not constant. What may be a luxury item for me may be a necessity for my wife. We have a growing family, and expenses are always changing. I am also readily aware that what we think we need to live on is so different from other parts of the world. But we work it out before God.

---

6. Craig L. Blomberg, *Preaching the Parables: From Responsible Interpretation to Powerful Proclamation* (Grand Rapids: Baker, 2004), 52.
7. Craig L. Blomberg, *Neither Poverty nor Riches: A Biblical Theology of Possessions*, New Studies in Biblical Theology vol. 7, ed. D. A. Carson (Downers Grove, IVP, 1999).

A Spiritual Barometer

I am not saying this is easy. My heart is so easily pulled away from being satisfied in Christ and toward being satisfied in possessions and lifestyle. I have to remind myself that the things I buy simply won't last and will not satisfy me. Life does not consist in the abundance of possessions; it consists in the abundance of God.

Our attachment to money says something about our devotion to God. "Where your treasure is, there your heart will be also" (Matt. 6:21). We will be devoted to what we treasure. If we treasure money, that's where our heart will be. Practically speaking if we treasure our house, our next shopping expedition, the stock market, our bank balance and so on, then our hearts will likewise be consumed with these things. If our treasure is Christ and his rule in our lives, however, then our hearts will be consumed by thoughts of building his Church and loving our neighbors by helping those who are lost and in need of Jesus.

Jesus uses the eyes as a metaphor for a spiritual barometer.

> The eye is the lamp of the body. If your eyes are good, your whole body will be full of light. But if your eyes are bad, your whole body will be full of darkness. If then the light within you is darkness, how great is that darkness! (Matt. 6:22–23).

The eye was thought to be the window into one's soul. Our eyes act as a lamp in that they shine light on what we treasure. You can tell a lot about a person's soul by what he spends his time looking at. If I spend a lot of time looking at myself in the mirror, for example, this shows I think a lot about myself. If I am always looking at my mutual funds performance, this is a good indication of what I treasure.

There is some debate as to how Jesus uses the terms "good" and "bad" here, but I think the meaning is relatively straightforward. Jesus compares "good" eyes and "bad" eyes. The term "good" literally means "single" or "undivided" and conveys the idea of being focused on a single thing. She who has a good eye is therefore undivided in her focus. A good eye sees clearly. It sees as God sees. The term "good" can also mean generous. So which is it? Is it an undivided eye or a generous eye? There's no reason it can't be both. The undivided eye is singularly focused on eternal things; storing up treasures in heaven. The person with a good eye serves only God, not money (Matt. 6:24). Since they are undivided in their commitment to God, they are also generous with their money in responding to the needs of the kingdom. They are singularly focused on storing up treasures in heaven.

In contrast the term "bad" could be taken as a divided eye. This would be the person who serves "both God and money" (Matt. 6:24). Or it could represent someone who is stingy with their money. One who is divided in their commitment to God will likewise be reserved in giving generously to the cause of the kingdom. The person with a bad eye has one foot in the world and one foot in the faith. They give to the "cause" while trying to maintain the lifestyle they are accustomed to. Jesus says that this cannot be done. "No one can serve two masters. Either he will hate the one and love the other, or he will be devoted to the one and despise the other. You cannot serve both God and Money" (Matt. 6:24).

We must either store up treasures in heaven or treasures on earth. We must have good eyes or bad eyes. There is no third option, so there are only two outcomes. Those with good eyes who store up treasures in heaven are "full of light" (Matt. 6:22). Those who have bad eyes and store up treasures on earth are "full of darkness" (Matt. 6:23). As usual in Scripture light and darkness are respective metaphors for whether one belongs to God or the devil (cf. Matt. 5:14; 8:12; 22:13; 25:30; Luke 16:8). One cannot store up treasures on earth and be saved.

Will Only The Poor Be In Heaven?

A Rich Man and a Poor Man

Jesus told a parable about "a rich man who . . . lived in luxury every day" (Luke 16:19). The next character in the parable is a poor man who lay at the rich man's gate. His name was Lazarus, "covered with sores and longing to eat what fell from the rich man's table. Even the dogs came and licked his sores" (Luke 16:20–21). He's a pathetic sight. He probably couldn't walk since he "laid" at the gate, obviously looking for help, even if it meant scrounging for a few leftovers. Doubtless, those listening to the parable would have considered the wealthy man blessed by God (cf. Prov. 31:22) and perhaps the poor man lazy, a drunkard, or a glutton (Prov. 10:4; 23:21).

Yet "the time came when the beggar died and the angels carried him to Abraham's side. The rich man also died and was buried. In hell, where he was in torment, he looked up and saw Abraham far away, with Lazarus by his side" (Luke 16:22–23). The great reversal: Lazarus is now being comforted in heaven while the rich man is being tormented in hell. The rich man who lived so sumptuously and had it so good in life now exists in a state of eternal "agony in this fire." He longed for Lazarus to come to him just "to dip the tip of his finger in water and cool [his] tongue" (Luke 16:24). He pleaded with Abraham, but to no avail. "Son, remember that in your lifetime you received your good things, while Lazarus received bad things, but now he is comforted here and you are in agony" (Luke 16:25).

Wealthy Christians

On the surface it may seem like Jesus is saying that the poor go to heaven and the rich go to hell. In Luke's gospel Jesus declared "Blessed are you who are *poor,* for yours is the kingdom of God"

(Luke 6:20). He goes on to state, "Woe to you who are *rich,* for you have already received your comfort" (Luke 6:24). Clearly, Jesus is speaking in economic categories since he would hardly be damning the spiritually rich! Jesus came and preached the gospel to those who were poor (Luke 4:18). Does this then mean that wealthy people will not be in heaven? No. Abraham, Jacob, Joseph, David and Daniel—to name a few—all seemed to be wealthy individuals. Job is perhaps the best example of a saint who was wealthy. In the New Testament Philemon must have been wealthy since he lived in a house big enough for the church to meet in. Likewise, Mary the mother of John Mark (Acts 12:12), Lydia (Acts 16:14, 40), Philip the evangelist (Acts 21:8), Mnason (Acts 21:16), Priscilla and Aquila (Rom. 16:5; 1 Cor. 16:19), Gaius (Rom. 16:23) and Nympha (Col 4:15) all seem to be wealthy Christians with largish houses.

I don't want to try and negate what Jesus has said about wealth, just to point out that wealthy Christians do exist, just as poor non-Christians obviously exist. Wealth itself has no bearing on where one spends eternity. That will be decided, as the rich man in this parable eventually did discover, albeit too late, by *repentance* (Luke 16:30).

The Real Issue—Repentance

Discovering the need for repentance indicates that those who are in heaven will indeed have "produce[d] fruit in keeping with repentance" (Luke 3:8). Fruit in keeping with repentance would be the man with two tunics sharing with him who has none, and the one who has food doing the same. This man doesn't collect any more than required, doesn't extort money, and is content with his pay (see Luke 3:8, 11, 13–14). While one may have wealth, Jesus thus urges Christians to use their wealth for kingdom purposes. This means that "it is impossible to be both rich and Christian without simultaneously being generous and sharing what we have with others."[8] No one will be excluded from heaven because they are wealthy. They will be excluded if they have been stingy with their wealth and lived in luxury while others have gone without. How can the love of God be in them (1 John 3:17)? Their stinginess is merely symptomatic of an absence of trust in God and a failure to grasp his immense love and kindness expressed in the gospel.

The rich man lived to excess and neglected the needs of Lazarus, whom he would have seen every day as he left his palatial homestead. "He was in a position to offer enormous help, but he refused to lift so much as a finger."[9] He even knew this beggar's name: "send *Lazarus* to dip the tip of his finger in water and cool my tongue" (Luke 16:24). Clearly, he was "a stingy man . . . eager to get rich and . . . unaware that poverty awaits him" (Prov. 28:22).

I was speaking to a "comfortably well off" man in a church last Sunday who told me that he would give his money to the poor if he could only find some! The poor he could find were not worthy in his mind to receive his money because they would waste the money on booze or drugs. I guess we do have to be careful. But it did strike me as odd, nonetheless, that a man evidently so keen to give away money to the poor could not find anyone to give it too. Did not Jesus say, "The poor you will always have with you" (Matt. 26:11; Mark 14:11)? They must be somewhere. In the rich man's case "the poor" was a man right at his gate. I suspect that they are not that far away from you and me either, if we will but open our eyes and look.

---

8. Blomberg, *Preaching the Parables*, 51.
9. Ibid., 50.

SALVATION IS MORE COMPLICATED THAN YOU THINK

ONE WEALTHY MAN WHO WON'T MAKE IT TO HEAVEN

An Evangelistic Opportunity Gone Awry?

A biblical literacy game: Ask a hundred people on the street about the "rich young ruler" in Jesus' encounter, and you might get two people who have a clue as to what you mean. A much higher percentage, though, are probably aware that Jesus said to someone, "sell everything you have and give to the poor and you will have treasure in heaven" (Mark 10:21; Luke 18:22; cf. Matt. 19:21). This saying has become axiomatic even in our wealth-driven culture, yet everywhere it goes unheeded.

Let's look at the statement itself. It seems an odd thing to say, especially since this was an evangelistic opportunity for Jesus! The first words out of the rich man's mouth are, "What must I do to inherit eternal life?" (Matt. 19:16; Mark 10:17; Luke 18:18). Don't you dream of opportunities like this? Jesus had a great chance to give this young man the gospel.

It reminds me of when I said to my friend years ago, "I don't think I'm a Christian. What do I need to do to become one?" I gave him this opportunity on a plate. And what did he say? "You just have to be committed!" For the longest time I thought he blew it.

This young, well-off legislator and/or blueblood comes to Jesus and asks what he must to do be saved, and Jesus basically tells him in no uncertain terms, "You just have to be committed!" He tells the young man to sell all his possessions and give the funds to the poor. If I thought my friend blew it then surely Jesus blew it. He didn't say "accept me into your heart, and you will have eternal life." We all know that Jesus didn't really blow it, right?

Outwardly Righteous

Only in Matthew's account does Jesus say, "If you want to enter life keep the commandments" (Matt. 19:17). This is clearly more than a little disturbing. Augustine makes it plain: "Note carefully that He did not say that he had only to believe and be baptized."[10] Does Jesus then require one to obey the law to have eternal life? Perhaps this is Jesus' means of evangelizing this man. In other words, he wants the man to see that in fact he hasn't kept the commandments, and indeed he can't keep them. The only way he can enter life is to acknowledge his problem and his need for a Savior. There is much that is attractive about this answer, but I wonder if it is too colored by our modern day practices and methods of evangelism. I think there is a better way to understand what Jesus is saying.

Notice that the rich ruler believes he has kept these commandments: "All these I have kept" (Matt. 19:20). But if this were the case, why does Jesus not grant him eternal life? The man still clearly lacked something (Luke 18:22).

Could it be this young man believed he had indeed obeyed these commands just like many other Jewish religious leaders in Jesus' day? When we look at some of the statements these people made, they don't look too bad—"I fast twice a week and give a tenth of all I get" (Luke 18:12); "You give a tenth of your spices—mint, dill and cumin. . . . You clean the outside of the cup and dish. . . . You . . . look beautiful on the outside. . . . On the outside you appear to people as righteous" (Matt. 23:23, 25, 27, 28). Pretty impressive! Of course, Jesus saw what people looking on could not; he saw their hearts. He saw that even though they appeared outwardly righteous, on the inside they were "full of hypocrisy and wickedness" (Matt. 23:28).

---

10. Augustine *Faith and Works* 13.20 (in *The Fathers of the Church: A New Translation*, ed. Joseph Deferrari, vol. 27 [New York: Fathers of the Church, 1955]).

This rich young ruler was no different. He had, in fact, obeyed these commandments, but he was still found lacking.

Justice, Mercy, and Faithfulness is Lacking

Even though the religious leaders were fastidious in their fasting, giving, praying and so forth, Jesus told them, "you have neglected the more important matters of the law—justice, mercy, and faithfulness. You should have practiced the latter, without neglecting the former" (Matt. 23:23). In other words, they still lacked something—justice, mercy, and faithfulness. This is now the direction Jesus takes the rich young ruler.

The ruler had neglected *justice* because his greed and love for money meant that the poor in his midst went without, while he had plenty. He neglected *mercy* because there was no way in first century Israel that he could have missed the many beggars that would have undoubtedly crossed his path seeking his help (cf. Matt. 26:11; Luke 16:20–21). And he neglected *faithfulness* because he failed to trust God and obey the many commands in the Old Testament to take care of the poor (e.g., Lev. 25:35; Deut. 15:4, 7, 11). This is the essence of what this man lacked.

But what about the command that follows? "Go, sell your possessions and give to the poor" (Matt. 19:21). What is it that this rich young ruler lacks? Isn't it clear? Doesn't Jesus spell it out in what he says next? "Sell everything you have and give to the poor." In other words, demonstrate justice, mercy and faithfulness.

I believe there are five very good reasons why Jesus commands the rich young ruler in this way, answering his question on how to inherit eternal life.

First, the opening question and Jesus' closing answer pertains to eternal life (Matt. 19:16, 28–29; cf. Mark 10:17, 30; Luke 18:18, 30). One would expect everything in the middle to, as well.

Second, Matthew's account clearly presents the command to sell all his possessions as the answer to what the ruler must do to enter life.

> Jesus: If you want to enter life, obey the commandments (Matt. 19:17).
>
> Ruler: All these I have kept. . . . What do I still lack? (Matt. 19:20).
>
> Jesus: If you want to be perfect, go, sell your possessions and give to the poor, and you will have treasure in heaven (Matt. 19:21).

Did you notice that verses 17 and 21 are asking and answering the *same* thing? "If you want to enter life" and "If you want to be perfect"? Perfection isn't something other than life; it is life itself. Remember that in the Sermon on the Mount to be "perfect"—not sinless—is to display surpassing righteousness, primarily characterized by love and mercy. Without surpassing righteousness no one can enter the kingdom of God. That is, no one can enter life.

Third, the rich young ruler is promised "treasure in heaven." We have seen in Matthew 6:19–24 that one who stores up treasures in heaven is "full of light" and saved. The rich young ruler has stored up treasures on earth. He is therefore a "fool" (Luke 12:20) and "full of darkness" (Matt. 6:23). "Misery" is coming upon him. His wealth will corrode and testify against him and eat his flesh like fire (James 5:1–3). To miss out on treasure in heaven is to miss out on heaven.

Fourth, Jesus understands the rich young ruler's failure to obey as a failure to enter the kingdom. This is obvious since immediately after the ruler left Jesus remarks on his decision, "I tell you the truth, it is hard for a rich man to enter the kingdom of heaven" (Matt. 19:22–23).

Fifth, the disciples understand Jesus to be talking about salvation. Notice how the conversation stays on topic once the ruler leaves.

When the young man heard this, he went away sad, because he had great wealth (Matt. 19:22).

Then Jesus said to his disciples, "I tell you the truth, it is hard for a rich man to enter the kingdom of heaven. Again I tell you, it is easier for a camel to go through the eye of a needle than for a rich man to enter the kingdom of God" (Matt. 19:23–24).

When the disciples heard this, they were greatly astonished and asked, "Who then can be *saved*?" (Matt. 19:25).

Prosperity Theology and the Command to Sell All?

Do we then need to sell our possessions and give to the poor in order to be saved? Is this the gospel for Jesus: "Sell all you have and you will be saved"?

We need to understand that the rich young ruler, like many Jews of his time, believed in the prosperity doctrine. In other words, "The rich will be saved." This man loved money. When he heard Jesus tell him to give it away he was very sad "*because* he had great wealth" (Matt. 19:22). His love for money was a barrier to inheriting eternal life.

A little background is important. It is well known[11] that one could selectively read the Old Testament and conclude that wealth was a sign of God's blessing. Abraham was "very wealthy" (Gen. 13:2). Isaac "reaped a hundredfold, because the Lord blessed him. The man became rich, and his wealth continued to grow until he became very wealthy" (Gen. 26:12–13). Jacob too became "exceedingly prosperous" (Gen. 30:43). Before Israel entered the land God declared through Moses,

---

11. See e.g., Warren Carter, *Households and Discipleship: A Study of Matthew 19–20,* Journal for the Study of the New Testament Supplement Series, 103, ed. Stanley E. Porter (Sheffield: Sheffield Academic Press, 1994), 131–38.

> If you fully obey the Lord your God and carefully follow all his commands . . . [t]he Lord will send a blessing on your barns and on everything you put your hand to. . . . The Lord will grant you abundant prosperity . . . in the land he swore to your forefathers to give you. . . . You will lend to many nations but will borrow from none (Deut. 28:1, 8, 11, 12).

It is not difficult to see how some would conclude, "If I am rich, then I am blessed by God." After all, the man who keeps away from sin and delights in God's law day and night will *prosper* (Ps. 1:3). The "man who fears the Lord, who finds great delight in his commands, . . . [w]ealth and riches are in his house" (Ps. 112:1, 3). If one who is rich is blessed, what must that mean for those who are poor? "He who ignores discipline comes to poverty and shame" (Prov. 13:18). No wonder Job's friend Eliphaz believed that the "vile and corrupt . . . the wicked man . . . [the one who] shakes his fist at God and vaunts himself against the Almighty . . . He will no longer be rich and his wealth will not endure, nor will his possessions spread over the land" (Job 15:16, 20, 25, 29).

It must have become very easy for people to make a connection between socio-economic status and God's blessing. Those who suffered must have done so because they were "worse sinners." Certainly not all believed that things were so cut and dried, but many did, and it seems that this rich young ruler was one of them. Not only him, though; it appears the disciples themselves harbored some prosperity mentality since they believed the rich man would be saved. On another occasion the disciples and Jesus came across a blind man, and the disciples asked Jesus, "Rabbi, who sinned, this man or his parents, that he was born blind?" (John 9:2).

Let's try and put ourselves in the disciples' minds. When they see a blind man, they automatically believe that he has been punished by God for sin. When they see a rich man, they conclude that his wealth is a sign of God's blessing. So when Jesus tells them that "it is hard for a rich man to enter the kingdom of heaven," they're flabbergasted. "*Who* then can be saved?" (Matt. 19:25), they question.

Child-like Faith in Jesus

The prosperity mentality is crucial for understanding this account. Because he knows what is in this ruler's heart (John 2:24–25), Jesus is actually asking the ruler to give up that which he is placing his *trust and confidence* in for salvation. If the ruler is to inherit eternal life, he is to place undivided faith in Jesus and believe that he alone is able to grant him treasure in heaven. After all, "whoever *believes* in [Jesus] shall not perish but have eternal life" (John 3:16). Jesus is not excluding rich people from the kingdom. He's simply saying, "No one can serve two masters. Either he will hate the one and love the other, or he will be devoted to the one and despise the other. You cannot serve [that is, trust] both God and Money" (Matt. 6:24).

The rich young ruler's problem was that he believed his wealth signified God's blessing on his life. According to his working theology, to give away his wealth would be to give away God's blessing and thus any hope of inheriting eternal life (to say nothing of life and comfort in the here and now). We can understand the man's dilemma. Jesus finishes by telling his disciples that the "many who are first will be last, and many who are last will be first" (Matt. 19:30). The rich ruler may have appeared blessed now, and the disciples who had given up everything might appear to be "last," but there would be a great reversal in eternity.

The primary lesson here is that Jesus requires us to place our undivided confidence and trust in him. This was the kind of faith Abraham exercised. He became "*fully persuaded* that God had power to do what he had promised" (Rom. 4:20). That's saving faith. The rich young ruler did not believe that Jesus had the power to do what he had promised—give him treasure in heaven—if he would sell all he had and give to the poor. Zane Hodges is absolutely right in this instance. What the rich young ruler lacked was indeed faith.[12] Hodges' and my point of departure is that I think the faith required here is inherently *trusting action*. It is no coincidence that immediately prior to this episode each Gospel writer includes the necessity of becoming like a child to enter the kingdom of God (Matt. 19:14; Mark 10:15; Luke 18:17). That says something: in refusing to sell his possessions and give to the poor, the rich young ruler lacked child-like faith.

Jesus does not ask everybody to sell *everything*. Jesus saves Zacchaeus in spite of his promising to give away *half* his possessions to the poor. Even so, Zacchaeus does promise to pay back four-fold to anyone he may have ripped off (Luke 19:1–9). This shows that what is important is the heart—which Jesus obviously sees (John 2:24–25). Zacchaeus was clearly willing to give everything away, and Jesus knew he meant it. God got the camel through the eye of a needle.

Actions Speak Louder Than Words

I have often heard it said that God is not against us having money and possessions, but he can be against our *attitude* towards them. In other words, the issue is not whether we have lots of money; the issue is whether in our minds the money we have belongs to God. I don't entirely disagree with this. The only problem is that I know my own heart, and it is a lot easier for me to say that my money is God's than actually to give it away. Sooner or later surely our belief that our money is God's must be tested. Concepts must inevitably give way to deeds. Actions speak louder than words!

If we're not careful we can so easily become like "the Pharisees, who loved money" (Luke 16:14). And Jesus said to them, "You are the ones who justify yourselves in the eyes of men, but God knows

---

12. Zane C. Hodges, *Absolutely Free: A Biblical Reply to Lordship Salvation* (Dallas: Rendención Viva, 1989), 186.

your hearts. What is highly valued among men is detestable in God's sight" (Luke 16:15). Is our belief that God is more concerned with our *attitude* toward wealth rather than our accumulation of it sometimes a way of justifying ourselves? We must always remember that whatever we might say to justify the money and possessions we have, God knows our hearts. "What is highly valued among men is detestable in God's sight."

Life does not consist in the abundance of our possessions. The widow who gave all she had to live on understood this (Mark 12:43–44). She did not know where her next meal would come from. She did not know how she would pay her bills. Some would say she was unwise to do what she did. Jesus didn't seem to think so. Life for her consisted in the abundance of God. She treasured God more than she treasured money and trusted God for her needs (Matt. 6:33). That's faith! What a fine example of devotion and love for God.

In his book *Preaching the Parables,* Craig Blomberg spends a chapter on a sermon he entitled "Can I Be Saved without Stewardship?" The question he's really asking is, "Can I be saved without generous Christian giving of many different kinds over a lifetime?" He answers, "I believe it's as logically impossible as saying we've experienced God's forgiveness without forgiving others, or that we know his love without loving others. He has been phenomenally generous in giving us eternal life, and when he has blessed us with material abundance on top of that, how can we not share generously from it if his Spirit truly dwells in us and guides us?"[13]

Jesus teaches in no uncertain terms that no one will enter into the riches of heaven who has not shared his riches with the poor here on earth. Let us be warned: we cannot be devoted to money and say we love God at the same time (Matt. 6:24), any more than we can say we love God and not others at the same time (1 John 4:20). We're lying in each case.

---

13. Blomberg, *Preaching the Parables,* 52.

CHAPTER EIGHT

CAN I BE SAVED AND NOT PERSEVERE?

I once heard a preacher tell of a person who had become a Christian and some time later that person decided he no longer wanted to be a Christian. The preacher told him something to the effect of, "Tough! Once a Christian, always a Christian. Even if you don't want to be a Christian, you are by virtue of your first decision."

Now to be fair, the point of the illustration, as I remember it, was to encourage us that God is faithful to his promises. Indeed he is: "If we are faithless, he will remain faithful, for he cannot disown himself" (2 Tim. 2:13). Praise God! Furthermore, I do not know the outcome of this illustration. Perhaps this new convert decided, "Well, if I'm a Christian whether I like it or not, I better get to living like one."

Was what this preacher said to this newly converted Christian correct? What happens if Christians decide they've had enough and stop believing? Are they still Christians? Were they ever Christians? These are questions we shall answer in this chapter.

The Need for Perseverance

What Does Jesus Say?

What would Jesus say to someone who decided they no longer wanted to follow him? We don't have to wonder; we know for sure. "He who stands firm (Greek = "perseveres") to the end will be saved" (Matt. 10:22). Augustine reminds us that Jesus did not say, "He who *begins* will be saved."[1] Jesus knows well that it is possible for some to "hear the word and at once receive it with joy. But since they have no root, they last only a short time. When trouble or persecution comes because of the word, they quickly fall away" (Mark 4:16–17). Strong and even joyful beginnings count for nothing if we do not last the distance.

Rather than tell someone who wants to give up on Jesus, "Once saved, always saved," we need to lovingly telling them, "He who stands firm to the end will be saved." It couldn't be clearer could it? Jesus is not talking in parables or riddles. His words are plain, so plain they hardly need explaining. Only those who persevere *to the end* will be saved. In other words, those who don't persevere to the end will *not* be saved.

Nevertheless, in spite of the clarity of these words—and that most commentators understand Jesus to be saying exactly what he appears to be saying—some see another meaning. Some understand Matthew 10:22 to be a reference to the necessity for Christians to persevere during the end-time tribulation. Perseverance is not necessary for salvation now *in the church age*, but it will be then *in the tribulation age*.

---

1. Augustine *Of the Agreement of the Evangelists Matthew and Luke in the Generations of the Lord* 1, in *Sermons on Selected Lessons of the New Testament*, A Library of Fathers of the Holy Catholic Church, Anterior to the Division of the East and the West, vol. 1 (Oxford: John Henry Parker, 1844).

This is no mere academic debate. The outcome of this discussion has serious implications for everybody who professes to trust in Jesus for salvation. If perseverance is necessary then the Christian life is not just a matter of waiting around for heaven. We are now called to "make every effort to enter through the narrow door" (Luke 13:24). Sunday sermons are no longer anecdotes of how to navigate the problems of life; they become the means by which we endure to the end and be saved (cf. 1 Tim. 4:16). Assurance no longer rests in a profession of the past but on whether we actively "listen" to Jesus' voice and "follow" him. For it is only to those who listen and follow that Jesus gives "eternal life, and they shall never perish; no one can snatch them out of [his] hand" (John 10:27–28).

Indeed things might look very different if we began to think less about "once saved always saved" and paid more attention to "he who stands firm to the end will be saved."

What Do The Epistles Say?

I am not going to defend the idea that Matthew 10:22 ("He who stands firm to the end will be saved") applies to Christians today; I have done this elsewhere.[2] I think the text is plain enough, and whether it refers to another age or not is irrelevant, for salvation is the same in every age (see Rom. 4). Furthermore, the New Testament epistles, clearly written for the church today, declare unequivocally that one must persevere to be saved.

> By this gospel you are saved, *if you hold firmly* to the word I preached to you. Otherwise, you have believed in vain (1 Cor. 15:2).
>
> But now he has reconciled you by Christ's physical body

---

2. See Alan P. Stanley, *Did Jesus Teach Salvation By Works: The Role of Works in Salvation in the Synoptic Gospels,* The Evangelical Theological Society Monograph Series, ed. David W. Baker, vol. 4 (Eugene, OR: Pickwick, 2006), 242–46.

through death to present you holy in his sight, without blemish and free from accusation—*if you continue* in your faith, established and firm, not moved from the hope held out in the gospel (Col. 1:22–23).

But Christ is faithful as a son over God's house. And we are his house, *if we hold on* to our courage and the hope of which we boast (Heb. 3:6).

And now, dear children, *continue in him, so that* when he appears we may be confident and unashamed before him at his coming (1 John 2:28).

It doesn't matter whether Matthew 10:22 refers to a tribulation period or not. We don't need Matthew 10:22; we have the rest of the New Testament. (Though it seems obvious to me that the New Testament writers got their idea of perseverance from Jesus!)

Perseverance Clarifies the Gospel

The implications should be obvious: "Continue to work out your salvation with fear and trembling" (Phil. 2:12); "Be all the more eager to make your calling and election sure" (2 Pet. 1:10); "Watch out that you do not lose what you have worked for, but that you may be rewarded fully" (2 John 8); for "to him who overcomes, I will give the right to eat from the tree of life, which is in the paradise of God" (Rev. 2:7).

This is the sole point of John Bunyan's *The Heavenly Footman: A Puritan's View on How To Get To Heaven:* "They that will have heaven must run for it."[3] In this light, he says, "Soul, I beseech thee, be serious."[4]

---

3. John Bunyan, *The Heavenly Footman: A Puritan's View of How to Get to Heaven* (Fearn, UK: Christian Heritage, 2002), 30.
4. Ibid., 63.

Perseverance is not an addition to the gospel. We are saved by grace through faith, and perseverance is not something extra tacked onto grace. Rather, perseverance *clarifies* the gospel. Quite simply, we must continue in and grow in the faith and repentance we expressed in the beginning.

> So then, *just as you received Christ Jesus as Lord, continue to live in him,* rooted and built up in him, strengthened in the faith as you were taught, and overflowing with thankfulness (Col. 2:6–7).
>
> We have come to share in Christ if we hold firmly till the end *the confidence we had at first* (Heb. 3:14).
>
> Let us hold firmly *to the faith we profess* (Heb. 4:14; cf. Heb. 10:23).

This doesn't mean that we continually "ask Jesus into our heart" day after day. But it does mean that we are to continue to trust in Christ and repent of our sins daily. Dependence is continual.

What Is Perseverance?

But what does it mean to stand firm; to persevere? Does it mean perseverance of mental assent, say, that Jesus is the only way to heaven? A while ago a concerned father told me of his son who was not "walking with the Lord." The father asked his son where he stood concerning God and matters pertaining to salvation. His son replied, "Sure dad, I still trust in Christ as my Savior." But is that all that is required to "stand firm to the end"?

Acknowledging Jesus Before Others

Jesus follows up his exhortation to stand firm to the end with a promise and a warning:

> Whoever acknowledges me before men, I will also acknowledge him before my Father in heaven. But whoever disowns me before men, I will disown him before my Father in heaven (Matt. 10:32–33; cf. Luke 12:8–9).

Jesus spoke these words in the midst of sending out his disciples to preach the gospel (Matt. 10:1–7). As they went out, he told them that they would face many obstacles. Some would simply not welcome them or their message (Matt. 10:14). But that would be the least of it. Some would hand them over to the local councils and flog them in their synagogues. On his account, they were brought before governors and kings (Matt. 10:17–18). They would be "persecuted" (Matt. 10:23) but they were not to "be afraid" (Matt. 10:26, 28, 31) for God cared for them (Matt. 10:29–31). Indeed they were to continue to "speak in the daylight," and they were to "proclaim from the roofs" the message of the gospel (Matt. 10:27). It wasn't easy. Jesus "did not come to bring peace, but a sword" (Matt. 10:34). Families would divide on account of the gospel (Matt. 10:35–36), but genuine disciples would love Jesus more than their own families, indeed more than their own lives (Matt. 10:35–39).

Jesus told his disciples that when they appeared before hostile authorities they should not fail to publicly acknowledge him. Those who failed to acknowledge him would find that Jesus will likewise not acknowledge them on the day of judgment: he will disown them.

What About Peter's Denial?

If those who fail to acknowledge Jesus will themselves be disowned by Jesus, then what do we make of Peter? Did he not fail to acknowledge Jesus before men, not once, but three times?

> Now Peter was sitting out in the courtyard, and a servant girl came to him. "You also were with Jesus of Galilee," she said.

Can I Be Saved and Not Persevere?

But *he denied it before them all.* "I don't know what you're talking about," he said . . . another girl saw him and said to the people there, "This fellow was with Jesus of Nazareth." *He denied it again, with an oath: "I don't know the man!"* After a little while, those standing there went up to Peter and said, "Surely you are one of them, for your accent gives you away." Then he began to call down curses on himself and he swore to them, *"I don't know the man!"* (Matt. 26:69–74).

What's remarkable about Peter's denial is that the wording in Greek matches Jesus' warning in Matthew 10:33.

Jesus: "whoever disowns (*arneomai*) me before (*emprosthen*) men" (Matt. 10:33)

Peter: "He denied (*arneomai*) it before (*emprosthen*) them all" (Matt. 26:70).

There is no doubt that Peter fits the category of Jesus' warning; in fact, he fits it three times! So did Peter get a special exemption, preferential treatment perhaps? Or does Jesus' warning allow for the occasional lapse?

Rather than thinking Peter got away with it, his three-fold denial is actually very helpful in understanding the nature of Jesus' warning. Obviously, Jesus' warning only applies to those who *continue* in a state of denying Jesus. (In other words, if Peter had continued in a state of denial, he would be in hell now). Judas is the prime example.

JUDAS VERSUS PETER

We can learn a lot about the nature of Peter's denial by comparing it with Judas' betrayal. Peter's intentions were sincere, whereas Judas flat out lied. Judas had already agreed on an amount of money to hand Jesus over to the authorities (Matt. 26:14–16) when Jesus told his disciples that one of them would betray him. Peter, who had *not yet* denied Jesus, exclaimed, "Surely not I, Lord?" (Matt. 26:22); "I will lay down my life for you" (John 13:37). Judas, on the other hand, who had *already* betrayed Jesus exclaimed, "Surely not I, Rabbi?" (Matt. 26:25). Judas deceived while we must assume that Peter's intentions at this point were sincere.

When the authorities finally came to arrest Jesus, Judas again lied and acted as though he loved Jesus, saying, "Greetings, Rabbi!" and kissing him (Matt. 26:49). What blatant hypocrisy. Two times he pretended to be loyal to Jesus. He was obviously a betrayer in his heart even though he didn't speak and act like one.

Peter demonstrates humble repentance while Judas demonstrates selfish repentance. Judas does feel sorry for what he has done and "was seized with remorse and returned the thirty silver coins to the chief priests and the elders" (Matt. 27:3). However, rather than running to Jesus and confessing his sin, "he went away and hanged himself" (Matt. 27:5). His sorrow did not lead him to true repentance. He merely felt bad for handing over an innocent man and simply couldn't live with himself.

Contrast this with Peter's response. He was clearly repentant in both word and action. First, he "remembered the word Jesus had spoken: 'Before the rooster crows, you will disown me three times'" (Matt. 26:75). Genuine repentance must always begin with being confronted by the truth of God's word. After David had committed adultery and murder, the prophet Nathan came to David and said, "You are the man! This is what the Lord, the God of Israel, says: 'I anointed you king over Israel . . . Why did you despise the word of the Lord by doing what is evil in his eyes? . . . Then David said to Nathan, 'I have sinned against the Lord'" (2 Sam. 12:7, 9, 13). David heard God's word and repented (Ps. 51).

Second, Peter mourned over his sin. When Peter recalled Jesus' words he wept bitterly. When David heard God's word through

Nathan, he too mourned, longing for relief from his sadness: "Let me hear *joy and gladness*; let the bones you have crushed *rejoice*. . . . Restore to me the *joy* of your salvation (Ps. 51:8, 12). Judas was remorseful, not because he had been confronted with God's word, but because he realized he had condemned an innocent man.

Third, the next time Peter saw Jesus he couldn't get to him fast enough (John 21:7–8). Contrast this response with Judas who went out and hanged himself. No doubt Peter felt bad, but he nevertheless ran to his Savior. Those who are truly repentant will doubtless feel like the tax collector who could not even look up to heaven; nevertheless, the tax collector still prayed to God (Luke 18:13). David, too, immediately after he had confessed his sin "pleaded with God" (2 Sam 12:16) and eventually "went into the house of the Lord and worshiped" (2 Sam. 12:20). If we do not go to God but wallow in self-pity, we have not truly repented.

Fourth, Peter affirmed his love for Jesus. Jesus followed up with an excruciating question and answer session—"Do you love me?" Peter nevertheless affirmed his love for Jesus—three times! (John 21:15–17).

There is a marked difference then between Peter's reaction to his denial and Judas' reaction to his betrayal. Of course, it is very significant that *before* Peter's denial's Jesus prayed for Peter, "that your faith may not fail" (Luke 22:32). So while Peter's faith may have suffered a set-back or three, *his faith did not fail!* This shows that Jesus' warning against denial in Matthew 10:33 is not a warning against momentary lapses of nerve, but against a settled denial of Jesus.

One final and important note: acknowledging Jesus before others is obviously not all about words. Judas acknowledged Jesus twice, once even with a kiss; you couldn't be more public about your affection for Jesus than that! Yet his heart was not where his lips were!

On the other hand Peter's heart was sincere and genuine though his words let him down at times.

Faith in the Gospel of John

Faith is central to the gospel of John. John wrote so "that you may *believe* that Jesus is the Christ, the Son of God, and that by believing you may have life in his name" (John 20:31). As we read through John, we see that "many *believed* in Jesus" (John 10:42). Jesus' "disciples put their *faith* in him" (John 2:11). Upon seeing his miracles "many people . . . *believed* in his name" (John 2:23). "Many of the Samaritans . . . *believed* in him" (John 4:39). A royal official "and all his household *believed*" (John 4:53). "Many in the crowd put their *faith* in him" (John 7:31). Some "Jews" *believed* in him (John 8:31; 12:11). A former blind man exclaimed, "Lord, I *believe*" (John 9:38). Martha told Jesus, "I *believe* that you are the Christ." (John 11:27). "Many even among the leaders *believed* in him" (John 12:42).

In spite of these many faith statements, we are never quite sure when a profession is genuine. For example, although the disciples believed early on we have no idea when they became "Christians." Philip, even after such a long time, does not appear to "know" Jesus (John 14:9). Late in his ministry, Jesus exclaims, "You believe at last!" (John 16:30–31; cf. 11:15). Yet a week or so later Thomas refuses to believe unless he can see Jesus' hands and side (John 20:25), and John does not believe until he sees inside the empty tomb (John 20:8). But earlier John tells us that it wasn't until after the resurrection that "they believed the Scripture and the words that Jesus had spoken" (John 2:22).

So when did the disciples become Christians? The answer is that we don't know. Indeed we are not meant to know; in John's gospel people believe in Jesus left, right, and center. And yet to some who believed, Jesus wouldn't entrust himself to them (John 2:23–25); others turned away (John 6:60); still others were said to "belong to [their] father, the devil" (John 8:44). Think about it! Some are still lost to Satan, some leave, Philip doesn't know, Peter denies, Thomas doubts, and Judas betrays. And yet all are "believers"! What are we to make of it all?

Remain in Me (John 15:1–6)

Fruit

John 15:4 states: "*Remain* in me, and I will remain in you." We must continually and deliberately keep trusting in Jesus.[5] Jesus draws on the imagery of horticulture to describe the relationship between himself and his disciples. Jesus is therefore "the true vine" meaning that he is the source of eternal life and fruitfulness; God the "Father is the gardener" (John 15:1); and the disciples "are the branches" (John 15:5). We must be in Jesus in order to produce fruit.

Cut Off

If we are unfruitful, we will be "cut off" (John 15:2). The word "cut off" is debated. It can mean "remove" or "lift up." It was common practice to *lift up* fallen vines into a position where they would be allowed to heal. Jesus could be saying that *fruitless* Christians are lifted up, encouraged, and put it into a position where they can

---

5. In fact I think there are good reasons for thinking that "Remain in me, and I will remain in you" is merely another way of saying, "He who stands firm to the end will be saved." The two passages in which these two verses occur (Matt. 10 and John 15) are strikingly similar (see Stanley, *Did Jesus Teach Salvation by Works*, 254–55). These similarities show that failure to stand firm to the end and not be saved is a failure to remain in Jesus, its result to be thrown into the fire and burned.

produce fruit. This is an attractive interpretation, but it does not fit with the imagery of John 15:6: "If anyone does not remain in me, he is like a branch that is thrown away and withers; such branches are picked up, thrown into the fire and burned." This is hardly a picture of lifted up and encouraged Christians. To think of a branch that is picked up and thrown into the fire is certainly to think of a branch that has been cut off.[6]

But what does it mean that a branch is cut off? I think what Jesus has in mind here is someone like Judas Iscariot who was by all appearances *in the vine*. In other words, someone who is cut off is someone that appeared to be in Jesus, but they never were. They called Jesus "Lord, Lord," they believed, they were baptized, they did miracles and cast out demons and all sorts of wonderful Christian things, but in the end Jesus will say he never knew them. We've already seen plenty of examples where people looked like Christians but weren't (e.g., Matt. 7:21–23; John 2:23–25; 6:60–66; 8:30–46; Acts 18:13). John himself dealt first hand with people who once appeared to be Christians but in hindsight proved they never were (1 John 2:19). To be "cut off" then is not, in my thinking anyway, to lose salvation but simply to demonstrate salvation was never present.

Remain in Me

Jesus says, "Remain in me, and I will remain in you" (John 15:4). The term "remain" is a favorite of John's, so it is not too hard to understand what it means. It basically means to "stay" (see John 2:12). But it has a deeper and richer theological meaning. Three

---

[6]. Furthermore, although the Greek word in question here *(airô)* does occur in John's Gospel to mean "lift up" (John 1:29; 2:16; 5:8–12; 8:59; 10:18, 24), it does not mean that after John 11. It means "cut off" (John 11:39, 41, 48; 16:22; 17:15; 19:15, 31, 38; 20:1, 2, 13, 15), suggesting that is what it means in John 15:2.

passages are important. The first is John 6:54, 56, which shows that to remain and to have eternal life are one and the same thing.

> Whoever eats my flesh and drinks my blood has *eternal life* (John 6:54).

> Whoever eats my flesh and drinks my blood *remains in me* and I in him (John 6:56).

John 17:3 tells us that "eternal life" means knowing the only true God, and Jesus Christ. If remaining in him means having eternal life, then to remain is to know God. In other words, to remain is to have a relationship, an ongoing relationship with God through Jesus Christ. After all, that's what a Christian is, isn't it—someone who has a personal relationship with God through Jesus Christ?

The second passage that sheds light on what it means to remain is John 8:30–31. To some Jews who believed, Jesus said, "If you hold (*remain*) to my teaching, you are really my disciples." To remain here "is a settled determination," writes George Beasley-Murray, "to live in and by . . . the word of Christ, followed by a perpetual listening to the word, reflecting on it, holding fast to it, and carrying out its command."[7]

The third passage that sheds light on the concept of "remaining" is John 15:5. Jesus says, "If a man remains in me and I in him, he will bear much fruit." Quite simply, remaining in Jesus will lead to producing fruit.

So what does Jesus mean when he says "remain in me"? He means to deliberately pursue an ongoing relationship with him. Such a relationship will involve listening to the word, meditating on it, clinging to it, and living in accordance with it, that is, producing fruit.

---

7. G. R. Beasley-Murray, *Gospel of Life: Theology in the Fourth Gospel* (Peabody, MA: Hendrickson, 1991), 107.

Fire and Burned

The fire imagery in John 15:6 suggests eternal rather than temporal judgment. Fire and hell go together. John the Baptist preached that those who did "not produce good *fruit* will be cut down and thrown into the *fire*" (Matt. 3:10). Jesus said that at the end of the age "the Son of Man will send out his angels, and they will weed out of his kingdom everything that causes sin and all who do evil. They will throw them into the *fiery* furnace, where there will be weeping and gnashing of teeth" (Matt. 13:41–42).

Here in John 15:6 Jesus is saying something strikingly similar: "If anyone does not remain in me, he is like a branch that is thrown away and withers; such branches are picked up, thrown into the *fire and burned*." The verse prior says that "If a man remains in me and I in him, he will bear much fruit" (John 15:5). By saying that those who don't remain will be thrown into the fire, verse six indicates that those who don't produce fruit will be thrown into the fire. This is exactly what John the Baptist warned would happen. And as we've seen before, this merely confirms that all Christians *will* produce fruit. Hell awaits those who don't.

Whoever *Continues* to Believe

The most well-known verse in the entire Bible is undoubtedly John 3:16: "For God so loved the world that he gave his one and only Son, that whoever *believes* in him shall not perish but have eternal life." Yet while it is well-known, it may well be the least understood. Most probably think this verse is expressing the need for a simple confession of faith in Jesus to receive eternal life, that thus we believe *once* and have eternal life.

Virtually all commentators on John's gospel, though, would agree that in keeping with the Greek present tense and John's theology, John 3:16 in fact means, "For God so loved the world that he gave his one and only Son, that whoever *continues to believe* in him shall not perish but have eternal life." Respected commentator Craig Keener interprets John 3:16 to mean that "one must develop the sort of faith that perseveres to the end."[8] Similarly, the late George Beasley-Murray, a world renown scholar in John Studies, regards "believe" in John 3:16 as something that "goes beyond a simple profession made in the presence of others; the Gospel emphasizes the necessity of continuing in faith and adhering to the word of Christ."[9]

Will Only A Few Be In Heaven?

Someone came to Jesus one day and asked him, "Lord, are only a few people going to be saved?" (Luke 13:23). The person was not asking, "Are only a few people going to become Christians?" Jesus answers:

> Make every effort to enter through the narrow door, because many, I tell you, will try to enter and will not be able to. Once the owner of the house gets up and closes the door, you will stand outside knocking and pleading, "Sir, open the door for us" (Luke 13:24–25).

We should make every effort to enter because there will be people standing outside of heaven trying to get in but won't be able to. Jesus will say to them, "I don't know you or where you come from" (Luke 13:25). Yet they will claim, "We ate and drank with you, and you taught in our streets" (Luke 13:26). Still Jesus will reply, "I don't know you or where you come from. Away from me, all you evildoers!" (Luke 13:27). They will stand outside in the darkness

---

8. Craig S. Keener, *The Gospel of John,* vol. 1 (Peabody, MA: Hendrickson, 2003), 570.
9. Beasley-Murray, *Gospel of Life,* 107.

expecting to be let in but instead they will be utterly shattered and "there will be weeping there, and gnashing of teeth" (Luke 13:28).

GRACE-PRODUCED EFFORT IS REQUIRED

Hence, Jesus says, "Make every effort to enter through the narrow door" (Luke 13:24). "Make every effort" is a translation of the Greek word *agônizomai*, from which we get the English word "agonize." The word means to *strain every nerve*.

The context in Luke 13 offers a couple of clues as to what Jesus means. First, he means more than simply seeking, for "many, I tell you, will *try* (Greek = "seek") to enter and will not be able to" (Luke 13:24). This implies that some effort, as opposed to mere seeking, is required. Second, "evildoers" will be refused entry into the kingdom (Luke 13:27). This implies that obedience and righteousness is required.

Outside of the gospels Paul uses *agônizomai* in contexts very similar to Luke 13. The strenuous effort required of athletes to gain a temporal crown is also required of Christians to gain "a crown that will last forever" (1 Cor. 9:25). Young Timothy must knuckle down and "train" himself to be godly because godliness has value for "the life to come . . . and for this we labor and *strive* (*agônizomai*)" (1 Tim. 4:7–8, 10). Timothy (as well as subsequent generations of Christians) is to labor and strive at being godly because this will prove valuable for the life to come. This will involve paying attention to speech, life, love, faith, purity and being devoted to God's word. We must be "diligent in these matters," giving ourselves "wholly" to them so that there might be "progress"; we must watch our "life and doctrine closely" and persevere in them (1 Tim. 4:12–16). Notice the verbs Paul uses: train, labor, devote, be diligent, give yourself wholly, watch, and persevere. Notice also the outcome: "if you do [these things], you will *save* both yourself and your hearers" (1 Tim. 4:16) in the life to come. Godliness is again the subject of 1 Timothy 6:12 where Paul urges Timothy to "*fight* (*agônizomai*) the good fight of the faith" by fleeing from sin, and pursuing "righteousness, godliness, faith, love, endurance, and gentleness." He must "take hold of the eternal life . . . until the appearing of our Lord Jesus Christ" (1 Tim. 6:11–14).

These few observations confirm and flesh out what Jesus meant by the term *agônizomai* in Luke 13. If we are to make every effort to enter through the narrow door we must diligently pursue godliness.[10] At first this sounds so contrary to grace until we remember that "the grace of God that brings salvation . . . teaches us to say 'no' to ungodliness and worldly passions, and to live self-controlled, upright and *godly* lives in this present age, while we wait for the blessed hope—the glorious appearing of our great God and Savior, Jesus Christ" (Titus 2:11–13).

Going the Distance

> Large crowds were traveling with Jesus, and turning to them he said: "If anyone comes to me and does not hate his father and mother, his wife and children, his brothers and sisters—yes, even his own life—he cannot be my disciple. And anyone who does not carry his cross and follow me cannot be my disciple. Suppose one of you wants to build a tower. Will he not first sit down and estimate the cost to see if he has enough money to complete it? For if he lays the foundation and is not able to finish it, everyone who sees it will ridicule him, saying, 'This fellow began to build and was not able to finish.' Or suppose

---

10. I. Howard Marshall, *The Gospel of Luke: A Commentary on the Greek Text*, The New International Greek Testament Commentary, ed. I. Howard Marshall and W. Ward Gasque (Grand Rapids: Eerdmans, 1978), 565: "moral effort is necessary in order to enter the kingdom."

a king is about to go to war against another king. Will he not first sit down and consider whether he is able with ten thousand men to oppose the one coming against him with twenty thousand? If he is not able, he will send a delegation while the other is still a long way off and will ask for terms of peace. In the same way, any of you who does not give up everything he has cannot be my disciple. Salt is good, but if it loses its saltiness, how can it be made salty again? It is fit neither for the soil nor for the manure pile; it is thrown out. He who has ears to hear, let him hear" (Luke 14:25–35).

Jesus is stressing here the need for perseverance. He makes his point a number of times. First, "anyone who does not . . . follow me cannot be my disciple." Second, "Will he not first sit down and estimate the cost to see if he has enough money to complete it?" Third, "Will he not first sit down and consider whether he is able with ten thousand men to oppose the one coming against him with twenty thousand?" Fourth, "any of you who does not give up everything he has cannot be my disciple." Fifth, "if [salt] loses its saltiness, how can it be made salty again? It is fit neither for the soil nor for the manure pile; it is thrown out."

Each of these statements conveys roughly the same point: discipleship entails commitment. We will look at each of these statements in turn.

Being a Disciple

In order to be a disciple we must put Jesus first in everything. Jesus says we must "hate" our own families. This paradoxical command is from the same Jesus who tells us to "love" our enemies, our wives, and one another. "By this all men will know that you are my disciples, if you *love* one another" (John 13:35). Disciples are to be characterized by love, not hate. It is quite clear Jesus does not mean that we should literally hate our families.

Matthew's version is in fact softer, though no less demanding: "Anyone who loves his father or mother more than me is not worthy of me; anyone who loves his son or daughter more than me is not worthy of me" (Matt. 10:37). We are to love our families, but we are to love Jesus more.

Demanding? Absolutely. But what else would we expect from One who "is the image of the invisible God, the firstborn over all creation," who created and sustains "all things," the "head" of the Church, the Supreme One (Col. 1:15–18)? The truth is that we'd be turned off if he was less demanding. Why is it that we tend to stay away from "cheap" stuff? Because we feel that those things that place a low demand on our wallet are inferior. When I was an agricultural consultant, we were told never to discount our services. Why? Because discounts would show that we had no confidence in our worth. God demands that we love him even more than those nearest and dearest to us. That tells us something about his worth. If Jesus said, "I want you to love me, but I understand if I have to play second fiddle to your family," we'd doubt his worth. So he tells us to love him more than anything and anyone. Why? Because he's worth more than anything or anyone.

Hence John Owen, English Puritan, wrote, "If what you are seeking is like Christ or equal to him, then reject Christ as one who has nothing desirable in him." Otherwise, "'Why do you spend your money for that which is not bread, and your labour for that which does not satisfy'"?[11] David said God's "love is better than life," so his "soul will be satisfied as with the richest of foods" (Ps. 63:3). Asaph said that "earth has nothing I desire but you" (Ps. 73:25).

We must love Jesus more because he is worth more.

---

11. John Owen, *Communion With God,* Treasures of John Owen for Today's Readers, ed. R. J. K. Law (Edinburgh, UK: Banner of Truth, 1991), 52.

Counting the Cost

This time two years ago I spent a week in Eastern Europe teaching. Across the road from where I was teaching there was a multi-storied building. Truthfully, one could hardly call it a building since there were no walls, floors, windows or ceilings. It was nothing but concrete in the shape of what was to be the police headquarters. They had run out of funds and were unable to finish. It looked derelict.

When a building stands half finished due to inadequate funds, people generally wonder why it was ever begun in the first place. They usually ridicule it and think that surely the wise thing would have been to sit down and estimate the cost to see if there was enough money to finish the task (see Luke 14:28). Unfinished projects are useless. We have a TV program here in Australia where a crew of builders and landscapers will visit a house where the husband—invariably it's the husband—has begun a project around the house. After years of nagging to no avail from his wife, she becomes fed up and writes to the program, and they come out and finish the job over a weekend.

An unfinished project is no use to anyone whether it's a building, home project, meal, race, hair-cut or whatever. So too an unfinished Christian is no use to God. They are unfit for heaven. This is not because they are unworthy. We are all unworthy. It is because they have not considered Jesus worthy.

But does this mean that before anyone can become a Christian they need to sit down and look ahead to see what will be involved and decide if they can go the distance? Certainly Jesus can't mean that we are to know in advance what we're in for. I look back to my "first" commitment and marvel at what I did not know. I had no idea—not even in principle—what I was in for.

Nevertheless, my experience is by no means a model. Jesus clearly says that "if we are not at least in principle prepared to surrender every area of our lives throughout our entire lives, then we are not making Jesus our 'Lord' or master above all human masters, including ourselves. In short, we are not becoming Christians."[12] This is something we often grow into.

Incurring Opposition

We soon discover that following Jesus is not a bed of roses. As we grow and learn and increasingly submit to him we understand that following him means opposition. At times it will feel like we are "ten thousand men" with "twenty thousand" coming against us (Luke 14:31).

Opposition comes because those who follow Jesus deny (Matt. 16:24) and humble themselves (Phil. 2:8); they please God and not people (Gal. 6:12); live contrary to the values and philosophies of this world (Gal. 6:14); and make choices and decisions that incur enemies (Phil. 3:18), insults (Mark 15:32), and persecution (Gal. 5:11), because to the world their choices appear foolish (1 Cor. 1:18) and offensive (Gal. 5:11).

My father is not a Christian. Even though my becoming a Christian did not please him, it probably did not bother him, at least until it impacted my decisions. The first one I remember is going on a missions trip to India for five weeks in 1990. It meant leaving on Christmas day—which meant no holiday time with my family. It also meant taking some leave from my work without pay. This was not a decision that my father applauded. Four years later I decided to leave my job and go to America to seminary. My dad wrote me for the first time pleading with my wife and me not to go. Of course, moving to Australia a decade later was not popular either, and being paid the way I am was even less popular. Even filling out tax-returns

---

12. Craig L. Blomberg, *Preaching the Parables: From Responsible Interpretation to Powerful Proclamation* (Grand Rapids: Baker, 2004), 184.

honestly has incurred some scorn. A couple of years ago my dad called me to ask me not to go to Eastern Europe because of some strife that was going on over there at the time.

The consequent lifestyle of taking up our cross and following Christ will not be popular. Not that we will all move to different countries and go to seminary and so on. Each one must take up *their* cross (cf. John 21:21–22; Gal. 6:4–5). Each of our lives will look different though they will be marked by commonalities—opposition, enemies, insult, and persecution. These marked Jesus' life, and it will be no different for those who follow him.

Giving Up Everything

Giving up "everything" (Luke 16:33) to be Jesus' disciple is to be viewed in light of what Christ offers. After all "if Jesus offers what he says he offers, then there can be no greater possession than following him."[13] Think about what he offers. He offers the kingdom of heaven: comfort, the earth, righteousness, mercy, seeing God, and being called sons of God (Matt. 5:4–9). There can be no greater possessions. No wonder Jesus speaks of the kingdom like "treasure hidden in a field" that "when a man found it, he hid it again, and then in his joy went and sold all he had and bought that field" (Matt. 13:44).

Practically though, what is Jesus saying here? Should we be selling everything? We like to qualify this, of course, by pointing out examples where people did not give up everything and yet became disciples. Zacchaeus is often cited (Luke 19:1–9). However as we've discussed even Zacchaeus, by promising to return fourfold what he had defrauded people, consciously put himself in a position where he knew he *might* have to give up everything.

---

13. Darrell L. Bock, *Luke 9:51–24:53*, Baker Exegetical Commentary on the New Testament, ed. Moisés Silva, vol. 2 (Grand Rapids: Baker, 1996), 1290.

Zacchaeus, I think, is a model of what it means to give up everything. Zacchaeus knew that money wouldn't satisfy and would quite happily give it all away for the sake of the kingdom. We are to live with a similar mindset. We are to live with the belief that nothing else will satisfy our souls except God. I believe this is the idea that Paul communicates when he says "those who buy something" should live as though "it were not theirs to keep; those who use the things of the world, as if not engrossed in them. For this world in its present form is passing away" (1 Cor. 7:30b–31). Our lives should demonstrate that our purchases and the things of this world are not the all-important and supreme element to our happiness, for "everything" is passing away.

A student of mine left her job as a school teacher to be a missionary in the Solomon Islands. But first she decided she needed to take three years to study at a Bible college. She has nearly finished her studies and will return to the Solomons soon. It is not difficult to see how she has given up everything. What impresses me is that she knows she will get malaria sometime since taking tablets long-term is not an option. She hasn't given up her health, but she knows at some time it will probably happen.

A very close friend of ours tells of how his grandparents in their younger days were very well off. It was the 1940s, and they lived on one of Sydney's up-market streets, owning a huge home offering panoramic views of the Parramatta River, the entrance to the pristine and elegant Sydney harbor. They also owned their own bakery business and a number of racing ponies. One night after one of their ponies won, they celebrated with a night out on the town. On their way home they came across a man on the corner of a major intersection of Sydney's downtown and stopped to hear him preach the gospel. They gave their lives to Christ then and there. They subsequently sold virtually everything they owned—their waterfront home, their race horses, and their business—the proceeds of which they gave to itinerant preachers and missionaries. From that point on they lived simply. Of course, we need not all be doing exactly what these people have done. But Jesus is saying that our lives must show somehow that our satisfaction is not in the things of this world but in Christ and his kingdom. Can people tell where your satisfaction is?

Are We Listening?

Jesus finishes with, "He who has ears to hear, let him hear" (Luke 14:35). Have we heard him? Have we taken seriously what he says? Bock says, "Jesus is not a minimalist when it comes to commitment."[14] It's either all or nothing. We are deceiving ourselves if we think we can still love Jesus yet not seriously embrace his demand on our lives. Of course, we are always growing in commitment. Remember, part of pursuing godliness is "progress." But it's one thing to grow in commitment and it's another to actively remain uncommitted. Excuses come so easily. "I just need to devote myself to my work for another two more years . . . get through university . . . earn some more money . . . wait until Christmas is over." In all our excuses, God gets second place.

If we still have excuses, what part of Jesus' words did we not hear or understand? Was it "if anyone comes to me and does not hate his father and mother . . . yes, even his own life—he cannot be my disciple"? Did we not hear "any of you who does not give up everything he has cannot be my disciple"? I believe Jesus would say, "Don't you get it? Don't you see? I'm worth more than anything else you could chase after. I love you, and I want you to love me—because I'm worth loving. I am more valuable than anything, and I won't be shared with anything or anyone. I won't come with you on your wide road. I won't blend into your worldly ways. I want none of it. If you

---

14. Ibid.

want me I'll live in you. There'll be work to do, but I'll take over. I want all of you. I want your time, money, family, attitudes, decision making criteria—I want it all—*I'm worth it!*"

Perseverance: Some Final Thoughts

Jesus' promise of salvation only applies to those who stand firm to the end, not to those who begin with a profession of faith. This means we must acknowledge Jesus before others, remembering that we are imperfect individuals who, like Peter, lack nerve at times. It means to continually and deliberately keep trusting in Jesus, cultivating an ongoing relationship with him through reading, reflecting, and following his Word in our daily lives. It means diligently and wholly devoting ourselves to the pursuit of godliness. Finally, it means going the distance. We must put Jesus first, loving him above all else, and not pulling out in spite of opposition.

Perseverance clarifies the essential elements of the gospel: faith and repentance. This is what it means to trust in Jesus and have an intimate relationship with him. Imagine the change that would take place if we balanced our preaching of "once saved always saved" with "he who stands firm to the end will be saved." Perhaps our churches would be healthier and dependent upon the grace of God as a result.

Indeed we all fail; we're imperfect. This is not about perfection; this is about perseverance. It seems we often want to accuse those who urge us on toward commitment and obedience of teaching something akin to sinless perfection. But this has nothing to do with sinless perfection. Perseverance is all about pursuing Christ and not giving up.

In fact, the very nature of endurance suggests that there will be setbacks and failures along the way. Just think of Jesus. He is held up as a model of perseverance (Heb. 12:2), yet prior to the cross he tells his disciples, "My soul is overwhelmed with sorrow to the point of death," then he prays, "My Father, if it is possible, may this cup be taken from me" (Matt. 26:38–39). While on the cross he cries out, "My God, my God, why have you forsaken me?" (Matt. 27:46). Does this sound like perseverance? I think that most of us think of perseverance as stoic determination with a grin-and-bear-it type attitude and emotional indifference, all for the cause of Christ. I have spoken with people going through deep suffering who feel that they have let God down because they cry.

Biblical perseverance is not a matter of exhibiting superhuman qualities in the midst of pain. We see Jesus emotionally engaged in his suffering. He feels and acknowledges the unpleasantness of it all. We distort the biblical concept of perseverance by imposing on it expectations that even Jesus did not meet. Suffering is a reminder of the reality of living in a fallen world, and it is not easy or pleasant.

Perseverance shines through when we hold on to God and trust him that his way his best; so we continue to live by his Word. That's what Jesus did. He delighted to do God's will (Heb. 10:7) and so prayed, "Yet not as I will, but as you will" (Matt. 26:39); thus "he entrusted himself to him who judges justly" (1 Pet. 2:23) and obeyed in the midst of suffering (Heb. 5:8).

As I write, a friend in my church has made me aware of a dear friend who has, so the doctors say, only two weeks to live. He has been battling cancer for twelve long years. In what appears to be his final email to his friends, he writes: "I am into the straight at this point. . . . The process of dying may be tedious—not particularly painful. But I am sure that Christ will go with me through the valley and receive me into glory. I have belonged to Him for fifty-odd years and He has never failed me. . . . My prayer is that Jesus be glorified in all this, and that those around me may know His loving support. . . . We are able to love Him with all our heart and soul-and mind-and strength. This wholeness I will take with me into the valley . . . [t]ill we meet again, at His feet . . ."

Many of Judah's kings provide a startling contrast to this gentleman dying of cancer and a sober warning to anyone who presumes that their Christian life will end the way it started. King Asa began so well, doing "what was good and right in the eyes of the Lord his God." Sadly, by the end of his life his heart had become astonishingly hardened to God and "even in his illness he did not seek help from the Lord" (2 Chron. 14–16). Joash lived much of his life doing "what was right in the eyes of the Lord," but ended his life as pagan as anyone (2 Chron. 24). Uzziah sought the Lord early on but later became unfaithful to God. Even "in his time of trouble King Ahaz became even more unfaithful to the Lord" (2 Chron. 28:22).

God will be the judge. We don't know the consequences of our fragility. It is a message to me that I must keep fixing my eyes on Jesus and pray that he "may sit at the helm and steer me safely; Suffer no adverse currents to divert my heavenward course; Let not my faith be wrecked amid storms and shoals. . . . The voyage is long, the waves high, the storms pitiless, but my helm is held steady. . . . Help me, protect me in the moving sea until I reach the shore of unceasing praise."[15]

---

15. Arthur Bennett, ed., *The Valley of Vision: A Collection of Puritan Prayers and Devotions* (Edinburgh: Banner of Truth, 1975), 110.

CHAPTER NINE

WILL GOD'S JUDGMENT AFFECT MY SALVATION?

I came across an interesting comment recently that unfortunately encapsulates a popular view of God today even amongst some Christians.

> I do believe in God. . . . Let me tell you about *my* God. My God is not vengeful, rather my God is my friend. My God is beautiful and loves me unconditionally, no matter what I do. My God doesn't judge me. How could God judge his own creation and call it bad? If he wanted us to do everything perfectly, He would have left us in a state of total perfection whence we came. But he gave us choice, and we can chose [sic.] whatever we want, and we can change our minds if we want. And that is not a sin, and we will got [sic.] be condemned for our choices, for this is the gift God gave to us, free will, and our choices gives [sic] us our experience, and makes us who we are . . . and more importantly . . . *who we chose to be*. My God loves me, no matter what.[1]

---

1. http://alyssadejour.blogspot.com/2005/06/what-hell.html (accessed 2:52 PM, December 12, 2006).

How could a loving God judge? For many, love and judgment are incompatible. Many also think that grace and works are incompatible, and we have seen clearly that they aren't.

Ever since the patriarchal days, God's people have thought of him as Judge (e.g., Gen. 16:5; 18:25; 31:53), looking forward to an appointed day (Ps. 75:2; Jer. 46:10) when "the Lord will judge the ends of the earth" (1 Sam. 2:10; cf. Gen. 18:25; 1 Chron. 16:33) in justice and righteousness (Ps. 9:8; 72:2; 96:10), when "the wicked will not stand in the judgment" (Ps. 1:5) while the righteous will "sing before the Lord" (Ps. 98:9) and be saved (Isa. 33:22).

When we come to the New Testament, we see many of these same themes repeated. John the Baptist proclaimed, "The ax is already at the root of the trees, and every tree that does not produce good fruit will be cut down and thrown into the fire" (Matt. 3:10). The New Testament writers also anticipate a time when God will "judge the world" (Rom. 3:6) on a set day though now through "the man he has appointed," "Jesus Christ" (Acts 17:31; Rom. 2:16). At that time *all* "the inhabitants of the earth" "will *all* stand before God's judgment seat" (Rev. 6:10; Rom. 14:10; cf. Heb. 12:23). God's people will be there (Heb. 10:30) since judgment begins "with the family of God" (1 Pet. 4:17). Those who reject God's Son will be condemned (John 12:48) while those who do not reject God's Son will not be condemned (John 5:24). "The Judge is standing at the door!" (James 5:9).

BE PREPARED

Judgment Will Count

I remember walking into my Ph.D. oral exam and one professor asked me, "How are you doing?" Another professor responded, "We'll be the judge of that!" That's quite true. We may think we're doing just fine now, or not, but there will come a day when the judge of all the earth will be the judge of that! It only makes sense to be prepared for that day. I turned up to a class one day and asked my students if they were ready for *the test*. They all looked at me in horror for there was no test scheduled for that day. I was playing with them a little; I wanted to test them on what they had been learning, but it wouldn't count toward their final mark. Oh, the relief on their faces.

We like to be prepared for tests and exams and things like that, whether it be a driver's license test or a football trial. No one likes to be caught off-guard, unless of course the test doesn't count for anything. Yet Jesus' judgment will count for all eternity. So would we not want to be prepared? It will be the greatest test we have ever faced. So why is it that many Christians seem to have such a cavalier attitude toward the day of judgment? Could it have anything to do with the "once saved always saved" idea and the presumption that our salvation won't be affected? What we have in our minds is a judgment that doesn't count—not for Christians anyway—and so we all breathe a sigh of relief.

It is true that Christians do not need to fear the day of judgment; we can be confident, but our confidence does not stem from a belief in "once saved always saved" mentality. It comes from the knowledge that "in this world we are like" Jesus (1 John 4:17). We must be prepared. After all, there are going to be well-meaning and sincere people who, while acknowledging Jesus as "Lord, Lord" and accomplishing all sorts of impressive spiritual feats, will sadly hear the words, "I never knew you. Away from me, you evildoers!" (Matt. 7:21–23). Try telling them afterward that Jesus' judgment didn't count. We must be prepared.

Prepared Means Being Faithful

As Jesus approaches the end of his time on earth, his disciples ask him a question concerning the signs of his coming at the "end of the age" (Matt. 24:3). Jesus tells them not to be concerned about the time but be faithful in the mean time (Matt. 24:4, 42, 44; 25:13). When Jesus returns he will be looking for faithful followers. Will he find them? (See Luke 18:8; cf. Matt. 24:45–46.) Exactly how disciples are to be faithful is the subject of the cluster of parables in Matthew 24:45–25:30.

The first parable of the faithful and wicked servants (Matt. 24:45–51) teaches that Jesus will bless those who have remained faithful to him. Being faithful simply means that we will have done what Jesus asked us to do. But if anyone gets tired of waiting and begins to live like an unbeliever (Matt. 24:49; cf. 1 Thess. 5:5–7), he will go to where unbelievers go. Jesus "will cut him to pieces and assign him a place with the hypocrites, where there will be weeping and gnashing of teeth" (Matt. 24:51). Those who say they want heaven and yet do not want to live like those who are going to heaven are not prepared; they are hypocrites.

The second parable of the ten virgins (Matt. 25:1–13) teaches that each person is individually responsible for whether they have been faithful or not.[2] So-called disciples who are caught off guard will not be able to shift the blame to anybody else. They will find the "door" of heaven "shut" to them in spite of their persistent pleading (Matt. 25:10). Because they didn't prepare for this day, Jesus will tell them, "I don't know you" (Matt. 25:12). We can't expect to appear before Jesus at judgment time and want him if we didn't want him on earth. What an insult! My students are never surprised when they get poor marks if they didn't prepare well. And yet some evidently will be confused over the reason why Jesus will shut them out of heaven.

The third parable of the talents (Matt. 25:14–30) teaches that we must be faithful with the various gifts and responsibilities that God has entrusted to us. In the parable a man gives his three

---

2. Darrell L. Bock, *Jesus According to Scripture: Restoring the Portrait from the Gospels* (Grand Rapids: Baker, 2002), 350.

servants five, two, and one talent respectively. The first two men responsibly put their money to work and double their money. On his return their master rewards them for their faithfulness, puts them "in charge of many things," and invites them to "come and share [their] master's happiness!" (Matt. 25:21, 23). The third servant, however, thinks his master is "a hard man" (Matt. 25:24) and so buries his talent in the ground. On his master's return, he scolds the servant for being "wicked" and "lazy" (Matt. 25:26). The talent is taken away from him, and "that worthless servant" is thrown "outside, into the darkness, where there will be weeping and gnashing of teeth" (Matt 25:30).

The lesson from the parable may not be readily apparent. We are not meant to think in terns of economics. Rather we should think about what it is that God has given us and what he expects from what he has given us. The New Testament teaches that Jesus has left his followers "each with his assigned task" (Mark 13:34). Each one has "different gifts, according to the grace given us" (Rom. 12:6), therefore "each one should carry his own load" (Gal. 6:5). We are simply "stewards" or "administrators." God has "entrusted" us and expects us to "prove faithful" (1 Cor. 4:1–2). It doesn't matter what the gift is, therefore, we are to be "faithfully *administering* God's grace in its various forms" (1 Pet. 4:10). This means using our gifts for the "common good" (1 Cor. 12:7) and serving others (1 Pet. 4:10). If we have a speaking gift we must speak faithfully as though it were God himself speaking. If we have a serving gift we should serve "with the strength God provides." Our ultimate aim is not self-glorification but "that in all things God may be praised through Jesus Christ" (1 Pet. 4:11). So, it doesn't matter if God has given us five gifts, two, or one, we are to be faithful stewards. Then at judgment time "each will receive his praise from God" (1 Cor. 4:5).

On the other hand, those who squander their gift(s) through lack of use or perhaps inappropriate use—boasting in their gifts as if they did not receive them from God (1Cor. 4:7) or selfishly using them to their own advantage or financial gain (cf. Acts 8:18–20; 1 Tim. 6:5; 1 Pet. 5:2)—will find the door of heaven closed to them. Be faithful with what God has given you.

The Basis For Judgment

Love and Mercy (The Sheep and the Goats)

But how will we be judged? What will the criteria be? What will be the outcome? Will our salvation be affected? Jesus provides a very clear answer to these questions in Matthew 25:31–46. The passage depicts the Son of Man sitting as judge "on his throne in heavenly glory" and "all the nations" of the world before him. Like a shepherd at a drafting gate separating sheep from goats, "he will separate the people one from another." The sheep will go to his right and the goats to his left (Matt. 25:31–33). The rest of the passage is simply a description of "how humanity will be separated."[3]

> Then the King will say to those on his right, "Come, you who are blessed by my Father; take your inheritance, the kingdom prepared for you since the creation of the world. For I was hungry and you gave me something to eat, I was thirsty and you gave me something to drink, I was a stranger and you invited me in, I needed clothes and you clothed me, I was sick and you looked after me, I was in prison and you came to visit me". . . . Then he will say to those on his left, "Depart from me, you who are cursed, into the eternal fire prepared for the devil and his angels. For I was hungry and you gave me nothing to eat, I was thirsty and you gave me nothing to drink, I was a stranger and you did not invite me in, I needed clothes

---

3. Ibid., 352.

and you did not clothe me, I was sick and in prison and you did not look after me". . . . Then they will go away to eternal punishment, but the righteous to eternal life (Matt 25:34–36, 41–43, 46).

Even though there is a long history of interpretation on this passage,[4] the general outline and content are not difficult for us to understand. This does not mean that this passage doesn't present difficulties. Along with Augustine we cannot help but notice that Christ "will not upbraid them because they did not believe in Him, but because they had not done good works."[5] Does this then not look "dangerously like justification by works"?[6] Juan Maldonado, a Spanish theologian, wrote in the sixteenth century, "If there were no other passage but this, it would be clear that eternal life is given not only after works but because of works, and is therefore truly and properly a reward."[7] Another has said that in "this whole passage there is no trace of a doctrine of the forgiveness of sins, or of the grace of God. The righteous are invited to enter into the Kingdom because they have shown themselves worthy by their kind deeds, not because their sins are forgiven. There is no trace of a saving *faith*. . . . There is no mercy shown to the accursed."[8] Finally, Craig Keener has said that this "passage explicitly declares that this judgment determines people's *eternal* destinies."[9] So what does this mean?

---

4. See Sherman W. Gray, *The Least of My Brothers, Matthew 25:31–46: A History of Interpretation*, Society of Biblical Literature Dissertation Series, ed. J. J. M. Roberts, vol. 114 (Atlanta: Scholars Press, 1989).
5. Augustine, *Faith and Works* 23.42 (in *The Fathers of the Church: A New Translation*, ed. Joseph Deferrari, vol. 27 [New York: Fathers of the Church, 1955]).
6. Michael Green, *Matthew for Today: Expository Study of Matthew* (Dallas: Word, 1988), 242.
7. Quoted in Gray, *The Least of My Brothers*, 201.
8. Francis Wright Beare, *The Gospel According to Matthew* (San Francisco: Harper & Row, 1981), 496–97.
9. Craig S. Keener, *A Commentary on the Gospel of Matthew* (Grand Rapids:

"Does acceptance of Jesus Christ by faith count for nothing at the end?"[10]

Understanding Jesus' Words

Before I answer this question here are some observations.

First, the majority of scholars rightly understand Jesus to be saying that all humanity will be judged—Jew, Gentile, believer, and unbeliever.[11] That "all the nations" (Matt. 25:32) will stand before Jesus does not mean that Jesus will judge countries but not people. Jesus has commissioned us to "make disciples of *all nations*" (Matt. 28:19), though he clearly expects us to make disciples of *people* (cf. Matt. 24:9, 14).

Second, just who are Jesus' "brothers" (Matt. 25:40)? Are they all Christians, people in the end-time tribulation, or merely any person in need, Christian or not? In spite of these views, their identity is not as difficult as what might first appear. The term "least" and "brother" in Matthew when not used to refer to blood brothers is a designation for disciples or followers of Jesus. For example, Jesus said, "whoever does the will of my Father in heaven is my *brother* and sister and mother" (Matt. 12:50), and to his disciples, "you are all *brothers*" (Matt. 23:8; cf. 18:15, 21, 35; 28:10).[12] Especially close to our passage in question is Matthew 10:42: "If anyone gives even a cup of cold water to one of *the least of these because he is my disciple,* I tell

---

Eerdmans, 1999), 604.
10. David Hill, *The Gospel of Matthew*, New Century Bible Commentary, ed. Ronald E. Clements and Matthew Black (Grand Rapids: Eerdmans, 1981), 330.
11. For the different interpretations offered by twentieth century authors on "all nations" see Gray, *The Least of My Brothers*, 257–67; W. D. Davies and Dale C. Allison, Jr., *A Critical and Exegetical Commentary on The Gospel According to Matthew*, International Critical Commentary, ed. J. A. Emerton, C. E. B. Cranfield, and G. N. Stanton, vol. 3 (Edinburgh: T & T Clark, 1997), 422.
12. Bock, *Jesus According to Scripture,* 353.

you the truth, he will certainly not lose his reward" (my translation). The "least of these" in Matthew 25:40 must therefore be a reference to all Christians.[13]

Third, we need to understand the sheep and goats judgment in light of Jesus' Great Commission. In other words Jesus commands his "brothers" (Christians) to take the gospel to the "sheep and goats" ("all nations"). As we all know people respond in all sorts of ways to Jesus' brothers who bring the gospel. But "he who receives you receives me, and he who receives me receives the one who sent me. . . . And if anyone gives even a cup of cold water to one of these little ones because he is my disciple, will certainly not lose his reward" (Matt. 10:40, 42).

Fourth, all who are Christians at the judgment (and thus brothers) were at one time goats. All those who are brothers will also be judged as people who belong to all the nations. We will all be judged for how we have treated God's people. "Therefore, as we have opportunity, let us do good to all people, especially to those who belong to the family of believers" (Gal. 6:10).

What About Faith?

Rather than counting for nothing, faith in Jesus Christ counts for everything come judgment day. The sheep and goat judgment simply demonstrates what Paul taught in Galatians 5:6: "The only thing that counts is faith expressing itself through love." As we have seen, it is impossible to be a Christian and not love others (1 John

---

13. Because of the similarities between Jesus' missionary discourse (Matt. 10) and the sheep and goats judgment, I think that "brothers" is more correctly to be understood as Christian missionaries. Yet since the Great Commission states that all Christians are to take the gospel to people, I don't see much difference, practically speaking.

4:20–21). Similarly, goats cannot say they love God and yet not show love to Jesus' brothers.

No one denies that believers will be judged on the basis of their works (e.g., 2 Cor. 5:10) although some suggest that what is at stake is not one's eternal destiny but rewards.[14] I do not have the space here to discuss rewards, so I will not even start.[15] What is very clear is that Jesus teaches that all humanity will be judged on the basis of their works and what will be at stake is their eternal destiny.

Paul teaches that God will judge all people on the basis of their works (Rom. 2:3–6): "To those who by persistence in doing good seek glory, honor and immortality, he will give eternal life. But for those who are self-seeking and who reject the truth and follow evil, there will be wrath and anger" (Rom. 2:7–8). What's hard to understand about that? "For of this you can be sure: No immoral, impure or greedy person . . . has any inheritance in the kingdom of Christ and of God" (Eph. 5:5). Aren't these words plain? These are not difficult passages. They may be difficult to swallow, but they are not difficult to understand. "Do not be deceived: God cannot be mocked. A man reaps what he sows. The one who sows to please his sinful nature, from that nature will reap destruction; the one who sows to please the Spirit, from the Spirit will reap eternal life. Let us not become

---

14. For a detailed articulation of this view see Joseph C. Dillow, *The Reign of the Servant Kings: A Study of Eternal Security and the Final Significance of Man* (Miami, FL: Schoettle, 1992), 1992; see also more recently Paul N. Benware, *The Believer's Payday: Why Standing before Christ Should Be Our Greatest Moment* (Chatanooga: AMG, 2002); Robert N. Wilkin, *The Road to Reward: Living Today in Light of Tomorrow* (Irving, TX: Grace Evangelical Society), 2003.
15. I have addressed the issue of rewards in Alan P. Stanley, *Did Jesus Teach Salvation By Works: The Role of Works in Salvation in the Synoptic Gospels,* The Evangelical Theological Society Monograph Series, ed. David W. Baker, vol. 4 (Eugene, OR: Pickwick, 2006), 273–81. On the subject of rewards I recommend Craig L. Blomberg, "Degrees of Reward in the Kingdom of Heaven?," *Journal of the Evangelical Theological Society* 35 (1992): 159–72; Thomas R. Schreiner and Ardel B. Caneday, *The Race Set Before Us: A Biblical Theology of Perseverance and Assurance* (Downers Grove: InterVarsity, 2001).

weary in doing good, for at the proper time we will reap a harvest if we do not give up" (Gal. 6:7–9). Augustine declared that "We must not imagine that any thoroughgoing scoundrel who remains utterly unreformed is likely to be received into" eternity—though of course no one knows "just what measure of unreformed immorality is compatible with God's mercy."[16]

But we must remember first things first. No one earns their way into eternity. If they did then those who have prophesied, driven out demons, and performed many miracles in the name of Jesus would be first through the gates. We have to turn everything on its head if we are going to say that now Jesus is suddenly teaching salvation by merit (see Matt. 9:9–13; 15:13; 18:23–27; 20:1–16; John 15:16).

We must bear in mind that when the New Testament is discussing the beginning of salvation, then things like grace, Jesus' call, faith, sinners and so forth get emphasized, but when the focus is on the end of salvation or eternity, things like works are the dominant focus. Knowledge of this fact alone should put many of the so-called "hard passages" concerning works and salvation in a more understandable light (e.g., Gal. 5:19–21; James 2:14–26).

Jesus gives a great example of this phenomenon at work in John 25:25–29 (see Figure 7 on the following page).

First things first then! Faith ("believes") first, *followed* by "good" works. Conversely, an absence of faith will be followed by "evil" works. Commenting on this passage, Augustine concludes, "Truly, the good life is inseparable from faith."[17] Similarly, James Arminius declared that, works "come into the judgment of God so far only as they are testimonies of faith."[18] John Wesley said it well, "All holiness must precede our entering into glory. But no holiness can exist, till,

---

16. Augustine, *City of God* 21.27 (in *The Fathers of the Church: A New Translation*, ed. Joseph Deferrari., vol. 14 [New York: Fathers of the Church, 1952]).
17. Augustine, *Faith and Works* 23.42.
18. James Arminius, *The Works of James Arminius,* trans. James Nichols, vol. 2 (Grand Rapids: Baker, 1986), 729.

'being justified by faith, we have peace with God, through our Lord Jesus Christ.'"[19]

FIGURE 7: FAITH FOLLOWED BY WORKS

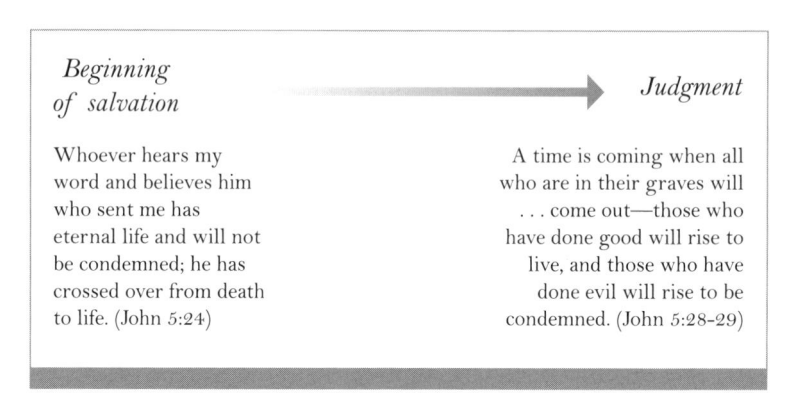

Beginning of salvation →	Judgment
Whoever hears my word and believes him who sent me has eternal life and will not be condemned; he has crossed over from death to life. (John 5:24)	A time is coming when all who are in their graves will . . . come out—those who have done good will rise to live, and those who have done evil will rise to be condemned. (John 5:28-29)

THE PURPOSE FOR JUDGMENT

Actions Reveal Our Priorities

But why have this judgment?[20] Why can't faith and absence of faith in Jesus be the criteria by which we are judged? Why does it have to be works? Presumably, the answer to that question has something to do with the fact that bogus Christians will be claiming occupancy rights in heaven (cf. Matt. 7:21–22). The judgment will show them how far they really were from being Christians, people

---

19. John Wesley, *The Works of John Wesley*, 1st ed., vol. 9 (London: Wesleyan Conference, 1872; reprint, Grand Rapids: Zondervan, 1958), 114.
20. We have over the course of this study actually looked at many other passages that discuss the day of judgment. I will simply reference them here: Matt. 7:1–2, 16–27; 10:32–33; Luke 3:11–14; 13:23–28; John 15:6.

who have personal relationships with Jesus Christ. Who belongs to the kingdom of heaven and who does not will be made fully known at the end of the age (Matt. 13:40, 49).[21]

An examination of our lives *will* reveal the true priorities of our heart; it's inevitable. Jesus taught that "from within, out of men's hearts, come evil thoughts, sexual immorality, theft, murder, adultery" and so on (Mark 7:21–22). It's a fact: bad trees don't produce good fruit and vice-versa. Thus, "a tree is recognized by its fruit" (Matt. 7:20; 12:33). It's the same with people. We can't help it. Eventually we act according to what we love and value (Matt. 12:35).

Nevertheless, we human beings are not always the best fruit inspectors. Jesus acknowledged that the church at Sardis had a reputation for being very much alive but in his judgment they were "dead" (Rev. 3:1). The Pharisees appeared to people as "clean" and "beautiful" and "righteous," yet in reality Jesus could see that they were greedy and selfish and wicked (Matt. 23:25, 27–28). We must "not be deceived: God cannot be mocked. A man reaps what he sows" (Gal. 6:7). We may deceive others and even ourselves, but on the day of judgment "wisdom is proved right by her actions" (Matt. 11:19).

Every Careless Word

Actions may speak louder than words but even our words will come under scrutiny at the judgment.

> I tell you that men will have to give account on the day of judgment for every careless word they have spoken. For by your words you will be acquitted, and by your words you will be condemned (Matt. 12:36–37).

We will all be held accountable for every careless word we have

---

21. Michael J. Wilkins, *Matthew*, The NIV Application Commentary Series, ed. Terry Muck (Grand Rapids: Zondervan, 2004), 493.

spoken. God knows every one of them, even those said in secret (Matt. 6:6). Jesus said that the mouth is the door by which all evil comes to expression (Matt. 15:11, 18–19). Hence, words are the manifestation of what's in our hearts. They will either *acquit* us or *condemn* us. The term *acquit* is the word "justify," the same word that Paul uses in Romans and Galatians. Yet Jesus uses the word here not to refer to our salvation at conversion but our salvation at the day of judgment (cf. James 2:20–26). Our words will therefore either justify—in the sense of vindicate or defend—the true condition of our hearts at the judgment, or they will condemn us to hell.

Is this fair? Isn't the issue faith in Jesus Christ? But Jesus is drawing on a sound principle here: just as good trees don't produce bad fruit, so too evil people don't "say anything good. . . . For out of the overflow of the heart the mouth speaks" (Matt. 12:34). Words reveal the true spiritual state of our heart. This doesn't mean that our mouths have to be full of blasphemy and profanity, though that will doubtless be the case with some. We shouldn't let the word "evil" mislead us into thinking Jesus means "bad" people. We already know that at the judgment many people will have done many things in Jesus' name yet nevertheless will be called "evil" (Matt. 7:23).

Jesus spoke this warning about careless words in the presence of the Pharisees who had just accused him of performing miracles by the power of Satan (Matt. 12:24). Yet we know that the Pharisees appeared righteous. They claimed that, "the only Father we have is God himself" (John 8:41). Like their forefathers, they would have cried out day and night, "O our God, we acknowledge you!" (Hos. 8:2). They cannot fool Jesus, though. To him they are a "brood of vipers . . . who are evil." They can't "say anything good. . . . For out of the overflow of the heart the mouth speaks" (Matt. 12:34).

Oh, how easily we can be deceived! We may utter prophesies in Jesus' name (Matt. 7:22), piously make promises to God (Matt. 15:5), even praise his name (James 3:9–10), and still have a heart that is in actuality never close to him, yet eventually hear the words, "I never knew you. Away from me, you evildoers!" (Matt. 7:23). The absence of "bad" talk and even the presence of "spiritual" talk does not guarantee acquittal on the day of judgment. The heart is always paramount.

How Do You Speak?

Words are like emails: once they're sent they can never be taken back. The Bible exhorts us to be careful how we speak. Perhaps the most obvious is that there should be no "obscenity, foolish talk or coarse joking, which are out of place, but rather thanksgiving" (Eph. 5:4). But there is a lot more to "Christian talk" than merely avoiding obscenities. Christians are to speak "the truth in love" (Eph. 4:15). We are never to put another person down—whether the information we have is true or false (James 4:11). Slandering in this way always involves harming another's reputation. We are therefore not to talk behind peoples' backs (Prov. 16:28). Rather we are to be promoters of love (Prov. 17:9).

If we have a problem with what comes out of our mouths, it is tempting to try and drum up ways in which to improve in this area. As helpful as this may or may not be, we should always remember that our words merely reflect our hearts. We need not to be thinking so much of our tongues but of our *hearts*. Have we *grasped* the heart of the gospel? Have we felt the weight of our sins now forgiven? Whether we tell lies, flatter or charm others, what comes out of the mouth is symptomatic of problems within the heart (Prov. 26:24–25, 28). People may not see it now, but the day of judgment will bring it to light. Be prepared.

CHAPTER TEN

SOME PASTORAL REFLECTIONS

During a Sunday night church service in Sydney in the 1960s, a violent thunder storm hit, and a massive lightening bolt hit the sandstone cross on the top of the church's roof. A huge lump of sandstone crashed through the roof and landed within inches of an unbelieving man. He was understandably very shaken and rattled off a few expletives, then he said, "If that's what God had to do to get my attention then he's got it 100 percent!" Before the night was over he received Christ and is still very active in Christian ministry in Sydney.

I am hoping that this book has been somewhat like that sandstone cross. I am hoping that God has your attention one hundred percent. Salvation is more complicated than you think! I hope you see that now. I do not mean complicated as in hard to understand. I mean complicated in terms of there being more to salvation than simply being "converted." The prevailing view amongst many Christians is that salvation is a moment in time faith decision, but that's a simplistic view of salvation. Salvation is not over until we reach the shores of heaven.

What Is a Christian?

In the remaining pages I want to address some of the questions we typically ask on this whole subject. These mainly concern assurance, eternal security, and the *level* of righteousness required to enter heaven. Before getting to these questions, though, I want to stress what I believe to be the most significant point of all: being a Christian is about having a personal relationship with God through his Son Jesus Christ. "Now this is eternal life: that they may *know* you, the only true God, and Jesus Christ, whom you have sent" (John 17:3). Jesus doesn't mean intellectual knowledge. He means an intimate and obedient relationship. God declares, "He defended the cause of the poor and needy. . . . Is that not what it means to *know* me?" (Jer. 22:16). "There is no faithfulness or steadfast love, and no *knowledge* of God in the land" (Hosea 4:1 ESV). "Be still, and *know* that I am God" (Ps. 46:10).

So what kind of intimate knowledge, though, does the Bible have in mind when it speaks of knowledge of the truth, knowledge that is eternal life, or the knowledge of God? God told Israel through the prophet Hosea that "There is no faithfulness or steadfast love, and no *knowledge* of God in the land" (Hosea 4:1 ESV). Knowledge of God consists of love for God and faithfulness to him. Israel lacked this kind of knowledge and was therefore "destroyed from lack of *knowledge.*" They "rejected *knowledge,*" thus God rejected them (Hosea 4:6).

Israel must therefore "return to the LORD" and "live in his presence." That's what it means to know the Lord, to "live in his presence." That kind of knowledge means that "as surely as the sun rises, he will appear; he will come to us like the winter rains, like the spring rains that water the earth" (Hosea 6:1–3). His coming to them will be as delightful as the winter and spring rains that water the earth.

Do you know God in this way? Do you *love* him intimately with your heart and not just your mind? Do you live in his presence and seek as David did to "set the Lord always before me" (Ps. 16:8)? Is his presence a delight to you, a refreshment, as satisfying as the rain on the earth? Not that we are there yet as Paul said: "I want to *know* Christ. . . . Not that I have already obtained all this, or have already been made perfect, but I press on. . . . I do not consider myself yet to have taken hold of it. But one thing I do: Forgetting what is behind and straining toward what is ahead, I press on toward the goal" (Phil. 3:10–14). So "let us *know* the Lord; let us press on to *know* him" (Hosea 6:3).

This has to be our number one pursuit: a relationship with God. God thus says, "Let not the wise man boast of his wisdom or the strong man boast of his strength or the rich man boast of his riches, but let him who boasts boast about this: that he understands and *knows* me, that I am the Lord" (Jer. 9:23–24). The big three pursuits of this world are wisdom, strength, or wealth. But they all originate "only in the flesh" (Jer. 9:25). The apostle Paul considered anything produced by the flesh "a loss compared to the surpassing greatness of *knowing* Christ Jesus my Lord" (Phil. 3:8). It's all "dung" he said (Phil. 3:8 kjv). That is all the flesh produces, dung! But a relationship with Jesus Christ is incomparable. Paul wanted "to *know* Christ" above all else (Phil. 3:10), and he wanted the same for his readers (Eph. 1:17). To know God is the only worthwhile and satisfying pursuit. Do you believe that?

To know him is God's expressed desire for humanity. He desired from his people "the *knowledge* of God rather than burnt offerings" (Hosea 6:6 esv) but they failed (Hos. 4:1). Therefore God promised to "give them a heart to *know* me, that I am the Lord" (Jer. 24:7). He "wants all men to be saved and to come to a *knowledge* of the truth" (1 Tim. 2:4). Now those who do not *know* God "will be punished with everlasting destruction and shut out from the presence of the Lord and from the majesty of his power" (2 Thess. 1:8–9). And those

Christ does not *know* will be excluded from the kingdom (Matt. 7:21–23).

All this simply means one thing: There is nothing more important than having a relationship with God through his Son Jesus Christ. But we *must* think in terms of *relationship,* not a decision or a profession of faith or a conversion experience or being baptized and so on—as important as these are. We all know what a relationship entails between close friends: connection, involvement, closeness, communication, listening and talking with each other, enjoyment, time, and so on. If we expect these things to characterize our earthly relationships, how much more should we expect these things in our relationship with God?

Making Sense of the Hard Questions

Progress

On the issue of works or a changed life or fruit—however we like to describe it—many ask, "How much is enough?" But this gets away from the issue of relationship. Some kind of standard or sinless perfection does not characterize the Christian life, progress does—"a hundred, sixty, or thirty times what was sown" (Matt. 13:23). There must be progress over the long haul. John Piper warns in this regard to "remember this: there is no standing still in the Christian life. Either we are advancing toward salvation, or we are drifting away to destruction. Drifting is mortal danger."[1]

Paul describes "those who live in accordance with the Spirit" as those who "have their minds set on what the Spirit desires" (Rom. 8:5). What he means is that Christians have a basic orientation

---

1. John Piper, *Brothers, We Are Not Professionals: A Plea to Pastors for Radical Ministry* (Nashville: Broadman and Holman, 2002), 109.

and direction about them. They are oriented toward the desires of the Spirit. They hunger and thirst for righteousness. They say with David, "The Lord is my light and my salvation.... Your face, Lord, I will seek" (Ps. 27:1, 8). This has nothing to do with perfection. David himself is troubled by sin for he pleads with God, "Do not hide your face from me, do not turn your servant away in anger.... Do not reject me or forsake me, O God my Savior" (Ps. 27:9).

Christians say with Paul, "I want to know Christ," and "not that I have already obtained all this, or have already been made perfect, but I press on to take hold of that for which Christ Jesus took hold of me" (Phil. 3:10, 12). There are three things to note about what Paul says here. One: his ultimate desire is to have a relationship with Christ. Two: he recognizes he's not there yet. For example, he gets a thorn in the flesh and his immediate reaction is not "your will be done" but "take it away Lord." Twice he reacts this way (2 Cor. 12:8). He's not perfect. Three: he recognizes that the Christian life is about progress and direction.

I have been a father now for five years, and looking for obedience in my children is a daily thing—and I mean *daily*. There are so many things to teach them—table manners, doing what we say when we say it, speaking nicely, treating one another kindly, sharing, and on it goes. I must admit that there are times when I feel like banging my head against a wall as I wonder whether they'll ever get it right. But most of the time I tend to take the long view. I think about where they have come from and where they are going. I am encouraged mostly because I see, not perfection, but progress.

Of course, in the Christian life I'm referring to grace-produced progress. "Are you so foolish? After beginning with the Spirit, are you now trying to attain your goal by human effort?" (Gal. 3:3). Unless it's grace-produced we will know nothing of the "rest for your souls" that Jesus promises those "who are weary and burdened" (Matt. 11:28–29). So the question, "how much is enough?" is misguided.

To think in these terms puts the emphasis back on works and righteousness rather than on a relationship with Christ. There are people who will stand at the judgment claiming that they have been good enough (Matt. 7:22). What is lacking, however, is not being "good enough" but a relationship with Christ.

The church at Ephesus had many good things going for it—"deeds," "hard work," "perseverance," and they could not "tolerate wicked men" (Rev. 2:2). Jesus holds one thing against them, however: they had forsaken their first love (Rev. 2:4). Their love for God and others had grown cold, and as a result they had slipped into mere orthodoxy. Thus Jesus warns them, "Remember the height from which you have fallen! Repent and do the things you did at first. If you do not repent, I will come to you and remove your lampstand from its place" (Rev. 2:5). How much more warning do we need on the importance of a loving relationship with God?

Assurance

If salvation entails a relationship, then we cannot give someone assurance of their salvation the moment they profess faith. The faith that makes someone a Christian is not limited to a moment in time.

Quite simply, the task of granting assurance is not ours. None of the apostles or New Testament writers ever assured their readers concerning their salvation; that job is always left up to the Holy Spirit (Rom. 8:16). The best that we can do is offer confidence (cf. 2 Tim. 1:5; Heb. 6:9).

First John is the classic book for assurance. If you want to know if you know God, you need to read 1 John. There you will find the following:

> We know that we have come to know him if we obey his commands (1 John 2:3).

> This is how we know we are in him: Whoever claims to live in him must walk as Jesus did (1 John 2:5–6).
>
> This is how we know who the children of God are and who the children of the devil are: Anyone who does not do what is right is not a child of God; nor is anyone who does not love his brother (1 John 3:10).
>
> We know that we have passed from death to life, because we love our brothers. Anyone who does not love remains in death (1 John 3:14).
>
> And this is how we know that he lives in us: We know it by the Spirit he gave us (1 John 3:24).

Who are we to think that we can provide a better answer to someone wanting assurance?

False Conversions

Rushing to give someone assurance ignores the reality of false conversions and misunderstands the role of discipleship.[2] Too often discipleship gets described as something that happens *after* salvation. The result is that many think of discipleship as an optional experience—one may become a Christian but opt out of discipleship. But this kind of thinking just does not square with the fact that Christians are "being saved" (1 Cor. 1:18; 2 Cor. 2:15).

---

2. I have addressed the role of discipleship in salvation in Alan P. Stanley, *Did Jesus Teach Salvation By Works: The Role of Works in Salvation in the Synoptic Gospels*, The Evangelical Theological Society Monograph Series, ed. David W. Baker, vol. 4 (Eugene, OR: Pickwick, 2006), 220–41. On the whole subject of discipleship, I recommend Michael J. Wilkins, *Following the Master: A Biblical Theology of Discipleship* (Grand Rapids: Zondervan, 1992).

Can I Lose My Salvation?

"Okay," I hear you say, "granted the existence of false conversions, but isn't salvation in its entirety automatic at the point of genuine conversion?" From God's point of view the answer is a resounding "yes" for "those he predestined, he also called; those he called, he also justified; those he justified, he also glorified" (Rom. 8:30). Conversion is vital. That's when we are "marked in him with a seal, the promised Holy Spirit, who is a deposit guaranteeing our inheritance" (Eph. 1:13–14).

But Scripture never allows us the luxury of resting in our conversion. If it did, then John would have simply reminded his readers of their initial profession of faith in Jesus to assure them that they have eternal life. Yet he doesn't do that. Rather he suggests that if certain things are not true of a person over the long haul they indicate that the person never came to know God in the first place. They haven't lost salvation; they simply never had it. This is the way John understands this issue, for he says that bogus Christians "went out from us, but they did not really belong to us. For if they had belonged to us, they would have remained with us; but their going showed that none of them belonged to us" (1 John 2:19). Hindsight indicates that these people were never Christians to begin with.

We must never think, therefore, that our conversion automatically means "safe!" If it did, then why did Paul bother to write, "I endure everything for the sake of the elect [people already converted], that they too may obtain the salvation that is in Christ Jesus, with eternal glory" (2 Tim. 2:10).[3] Paul is persuaded that Timothy is a genuine believer (2 Tim. 1:5), yet he still encourages him to watch his life and doctrine closely and to "persevere in them, because if you do, you will save both yourself and your hearers" (1 Tim. 4:16). The

---

3. See John Piper, *Brothers, We Are Not Professionals,* 105–111.

possibility always exists that believers may shipwreck their faith (e.g., 1 Tim. 1:19; 4:1; 6:10, 21).

We must "continue to work out [our] salvation with fear and trembling" (Phil. 2:12) and "be all the more eager to make [our] calling and election sure" so that we "will receive a rich welcome into the eternal kingdom of our Lord and Savior Jesus Christ" (2 Pet. 1:10–11). We are to *fear and tremble* and be *all the more eager,* not because we run the risk of losing our salvation but because it is only in this way that our calling and election are confirmed.[4] Christians then are to be characterized by prayerfulness and dependence upon the grace and mercy of God day after day for "God opposes the proud but gives [enabling] grace to the humble" (James 4:6). We must not presume to be standing firm lest we fall (1 Cor. 10:12).

I only just recently heard of a couple whose marriage had split up after forty years or so. I was good friends with their sons in primary school when they, the parents, would have been in their thirties. I would never have guessed that thirty years later they would be apart. Whenever I hear of a story like that I am reminded of my own vulnerability and helplessness as a husband. Who's to say that my marriage will last another thirty years? My only recourse is to come before God in prayer and plead for his grace and perseverance. I never presume that it will not happen to me.

It's no different in the Christian life. Who's to say that I will not shipwreck my faith? And even if I don't who's to say that I might not be standing before Jesus saying, "Lord, Lord," and hearing the words, "Away from me, . . . I never knew you"? Some might react to this by thinking, "Well, I better get working." My first thought is, "I better get praying," "for it is God who works in [me] to will and

---

4. On the delicate relationship between assurance, eternal security and the necessity for perseverance in the Christian life, I recommend the excellent work of Thomas R. Schreiner and Ardel B. Caneday, *The Race Set Before Us: A Biblical Theology of Perseverance and Assurance* (Downers Grove: InterVarsity, 2001).

to act according to his good purpose" (Phil 2:13). I must have God's enablement.

Satan had asked to "sift" Peter. He wanted to put him through his sieve and squeeze every ounce of faith out of him so that he would come through the other side destined for hell (Luke 22:31). The only reason Peter only denied Christ three times and not three million times is because Jesus had prayed for him that his "faith may not fail" (Luke 22:32). Beware! We can be sure of one thing: Satan will ask to sift us to show that our faith was never genuine in the first place. We must "watch and pray so" as to "not fall into temptation" (Matt. 26:41). We must "take [our] stand against the devil's schemes" (Eph. 6:11).

The reality of bogus Christians exposes the error of living by the "once saved always saved" mentality. We never find such a statement in Scripture. Instead what we find is, "he who stands firm to the end will be saved" (Matt. 10:22). Therefore "our eternal security should be focused not on remote past actions but on our present attitude toward Christ."[5]

What About Sin?

This doesn't mean that we look for perfection. There are a multitude of examples that we can look to in order to console ourselves that sin is not incompatible with being a Christian (e.g., Abraham, Moses, David, Peter).

There is, however, a vast difference between someone who looks to these examples to console their battle-wearied soul in their fight against sin and someone who uses them to merely justify and continue in their sinful habits. "Yes, the saints have their sins," writes Puritan Jeremiah Burroughs, "but how are they affected with them?"[6] That

---

5. Will Metzger, *Tell The Truth: The Whole Gospel to the Whole Person by Whole People,* revised edition (Downers Grove: IVP, 2002), 81.
6. Jeremiah Burroughs, *Hope,* ed. Don Kistler (Orlando, FL: Soli Deo Gloria, 2005), 42.

is the question. How does your sin affect you? "Does your remaining sin make you seek God and account yourself in the most wretched condition because of it."?[7] Are you poor in spirit, do you mourn, are you meek, and do you hunger and thirst for righteousness?

Think of Peter walking on water. When Peter began to sink he cried out to Jesus, "Lord, save me!" (Matt. 14:30). When we sin, do we cry out to God, "Lord, save me!" or are we content to let ourselves sink or try and pull ourselves up by our own strength? The notable point about Peter is not that he sank but that he cried out to Jesus in the midst of his sinking. That's what Christians do. That's what set David apart from Saul and Peter apart from Judas. All four sinned. All four demonstrated repentance to some extent, but only David and Peter genuinely cried out to God for mercy. C. S. Lewis wrote, "A Christian is not a man who never goes wrong, but a man who is enabled to repent and pick himself up and begin over again after each stumble."[8]

Christians are well aware of their sin. We "groan inwardly as we wait eagerly for our adoption as sons, the redemption of our bodies" (Rom. 8:23). This is a paradox of sorts. Christians make progress in holiness, yet the more progress they make the more aware of their sin they become. This was certainly Paul's experience concluding at the close of his life that, "Christ Jesus came into the world to save sinners—of whom I am the *worst*" (1 Tim. 1:15). When Isaiah stood in the presence of a holy God, he declared himself to be "a man of unclean lips" (Isa. 6:5). When Peter became aware that he was standing in the midst of divinity, he exclaimed, "Go away from me, Lord; I am a sinful man!" (Luke 5:8). This phenomenon is well known. C. S. Lewis observed "that the holier a man is, the more fully he is aware" of how horrible his character is to God.[9]

---

7. Ibid.
8. C. S. Lewis, *Mere Christianity* (London: Fount, 1997), 52.
9. C. S. Lewis, *The Problem of Pain* (London: Fontana, 1957), 55.

This paradox is explained by the nature of someone who is making progress in their Christian life. It is only the humble—the poor in spirit, and so forth—that make progress; yet they can hardly bear to look to heaven and so plead, "God, have mercy on me, a sinner."

We Are Not What We Should Be

It is quite obvious that "what we will be has not yet been made known. But we know that when he appears, we shall be like him, for we shall see him as he is" (1 John 3:2). So Christians live with hope. Not the kind of hope that the weather will be fine tomorrow but a sure hope, as sure as the sun *will* come up tomorrow. We shall one day see him as he is, and we will be like him. The key question is, what does this hope produce in you? Do you now "change the grace of our God into a license for immorality" (Jude 4)? Do you sin "because we are not under law but under grace" (Rom. 6:15)? Do you "use your freedom to indulge the sinful nature" (Gal. 5:13)? John says that everyone who has this hope in him purifies himself" (1 John 3:3). He does not say that everyone who has this hope in him keeps on sinning or becomes sluggish and apathetic. Someone who professes to have this hope yet cares little about growing in holiness has to question whether they are genuinely saved.

We Can So Easily Be Deceived

We must watch and pray against all manner of deception. The Israelites carried on their religiosity, but it was all a farce. Lest we think their religiosity was something we would never fall into, listen to the words of God through his prophet Isaiah:

> Declare to my people their rebellion and to the house of Jacob their sins. For day after day they seek me out; they seem eager to know my ways, as if they were a nation that does what is

right and has not forsaken the commands of its God. They ask me for just decisions and seem eager for God to come near them. "Why have we fasted," they say, "and you have not seen it? Why have we humbled ourselves, and you have not noticed?" (Isa. 58:1–4).

We often think of Old Testament Israel as outright apostates who blatantly turned their backs on God. Yet I am sure Israel never thought that way about themselves. After all, at least at some level of sincerity they *sought* God out, they seemed *eager* to know his ways, *eager* for God to come near, they *fasted* and *humbled* themselves. Could that be said of you? Are you eager to seek God and for him to be close to you? I am! Yet in Israel's case this was nothing more than rebellion and sin because when they did fast, they did what they pleased (see Isa. 58:4). A friend of mine calls this "compartmentalized Christianity." In other words, we make time for devotions, church, Bible study, prayer; we call Jesus "Lord, Lord" and do wonderful things, all in his name, and the rest of the time we do as we please. We give ten percent of our time and money to God, but the rest is ours. We can even say we have persevered. But we do as we please. We have forsaken our first love. We do not know Jesus, and he does not know us. We are deceived!

We can do all manner of "Christian" things and still "somehow be led astray from [our] sincere and pure devotion to Christ" (2 Cor. 11:3). Claims are cheap (see e.g., Gal. 6:3; James 1:22, 26; 2:14; 1 John 1:8)! We must "come into contact with Jesus," says Charles Spurgeon. False converts are people "who do not come into contact with Jesus. They are outward, external hearers only, but there is no inward touching of the blessed person of Christ, no spiritual contact with the ever blessed Savior, no stream of life and love flowing from Him to them. It is all mechanical religion."[10]

---

10. Charles Spurgeon, *Joy In Christ's Presence* (New Kensington, PA: Whitaker,

SALVATION IS MORE COMPLICATED THAN YOU THINK

> [They] come to the house of prayer and try to enter into the service. ... They may come to the Lord's Table. They may even join the church. They are baptized, yet not by the Holy Spirit. They take Communion, but they do not take the Lord Himself; they eat the bread, but they never eat His flesh; they drink the wine, but they never drink His blood. They have been immersed in water, but they have never been buried with Christ in baptism, nor have they risen again with Him into newness of life. To them, reading, singing, kneeling, hearing, and so on, are enough. They are content with the shell, but they know nothing of the blessed spiritual kernel, the true *'marrow and fatness'* (Ps. 63:5)."[11]

They are deceived!

Eternal Security

For this reason we must always return to grace. God is the only one "who is able to keep you from falling and to present you before his glorious presence without fault and with great joy" (Jude 24). This does not mean he is able to keep you but he might not; he *will* keep his people from falling. Part of the New Covenant promise to believers is that God "*will* give them singleness of heart and action, so that they *will* always fear me for their own good and the good of their children after them" (Jer. 32:39). What a wonderful promise. If there is any singleness of heart and action and fear of God in your life, it is only because God is putting it there and keeping it there. Yes, there are sins and failures and days when we are far from God. But over the course of our lives God is giving us the gift of singleness of heart and action and an appropriate fear of him.

Thus Jesus "is able to save *completely* those who come to God through him, because he always lives to intercede for them" (Heb.

1997), 152.
11. Ibid., 151–52.

7:25). Satan is asking to have you just like Peter, but Jesus is praying that your faith might not fail. By faith you are "shielded by God's power until the coming of the salvation that is ready to be revealed in the last time" (1 Pet. 1:5). God is working for your good to conform you into "the likeness of his Son"; he chose you, called you and justified you; he will glorify you, too. God is for you. Nothing will separate you from his love (Rom. 8:28–39). He will finish what he began in you (Phil. 1:6).

How do we reconcile these promises with the reality of false converts? The answer is that one may react to these promises in two ways. One may read them and think that on the basis of their profession of faith they have nothing to worry about—once saved always saved! They may exist as a Christian in some sense doing the Christian "stuff" but never appreciating the urgency that is required to make their calling and election sure. This type of person may in fact be lost because he was never saved in the first place.

Another person may read these promises and take great encouragement that God will transform this wretched sinner and conform him over time into the likeness of Christ. He prays God's promises back to him and asks that God would indeed save him completely. He asks that God would finish what he began and conform him to the likeness of Christ. He pleads with God that he himself would give him a singleness of heart and action and a fear of the Lord. He thanks God for his mercy and grace and knows that the only reason he awakes in the morning with a desire for him is because of his gracious enablement.

EXAMINATION AND URGENCY REQUIRED

The book of Malachi was the last Old Testament book written. The people were back in the land, the temple had been restored, and the city walls were back up. Nothing much was happening on any front.

Life merely went on. But the end of the age had not come as expected, and Israel was simply going through the motions. They neither feared nor honored God (Mal. 1:6) and in fact found the whole business of worshiping him quite burdensome (Mal. 1:13). Nevertheless, they did worship even though their hearts weren't in it.

What's amazing about all this is that Israel appears to have absolutely *no idea* that they are offending God. They're thick! God tells the priests they are treating him with contempt. They're flabbergasted and ask, "How have we shown contempt for your name?" (Mal. 1:6). They have used defiled food on the altar, yet they ask, "How have we defiled you?" (Mal. 1:7). They're clueless. They have wearied God, but they can't see how: "How have we wearied him?" (Mal. 2:17). They aren't even aware they need to return to God: "How are we to return?" (Mal. 3:7). "How do we rob you?" (Mal. 3:8); "What have we said against you?" (Mal. 3:14) and on it goes! How remarkable: they don't have any idea that they are offside with God.

If God sent a prophet to you or your church and told you that you were treating him with contempt, would you stand there aghast and ask, "How?" If he told you to return, would you wonder how you had ever been away? Is it possible that you are deceiving yourself? We must examine ourselves. He is "'a great king,' says the Lord Almighty, 'and my name is to be feared among the nations'" (Mal. 1:14).

A student asked me a couple of years ago why there was such a lack of urgency in the Church today. "Could it be," I contemplated, "that we don't feel as though we have anything to be urgent about?" If that's so, it's not the opinion of the New Testament writers, and it's certainly not the opinion of Jesus. We must be urgent. Eternity hinges on grace-produced, God-motivated, Spirit-saturated, Christ-centered urgency. "Make every effort to enter through the narrow door, because many, I tell you, will try to enter and will not be able to" (Luke 13:24).

Yes, indeed we must be urgent. We must "see to it that no one," including ourselves, "misses the grace of God" (Heb. 12:15). *Know* God "and serve him with wholehearted devotion and with a willing mind, for the Lord searches every heart and understands every motive behind the thoughts. If you seek him, he will be found by you; but if you forsake him, he will reject you forever" (1 Chron. 28:9).